Peterhof • See the magnificent Grand Cascade fountain at the 'Russian Versailles' *(page 75)*

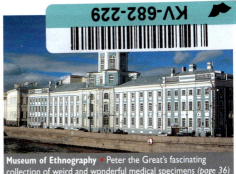

Museum of Ethnography • Peter the Great's fascinating collection of weird and wonderful medical specimens *(page 36)*

Winter Palace and Hermitage • A vast treasure trove of art collected over centuries by the Russian royal family *(page 42)*

Piskaryovskoe Cemetery • A sombre memorial to the victims of the blockade *(page 73)*

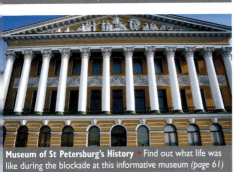

Museum of St Petersburg's History • Find out what life was like during the blockade at this informative museum *(page 61)*

Yusupov Palace • The lavish interior is preserved exactly as it was when the wealthy Yusupovs lived here *(page 65)*

KV-682-229

77

85

10

CONTENTS

78

28

103

INTRODUCTION

After nearly a century of destruction and neglect, St Petersburg is once again emerging as Russia's most beautiful city. Founded by Peter the Great in 1703 on the marshy banks of the Neva river, the city was built as a 'window onto Europe' and as the modern successor to the old capital of Moscow. Built on 44 islands set among canals and rivers and crossed by over 300 bridges, it is rightfully called the 'Venice of the North': a city where pastel-coloured palaces are reflected in the canals, where mansions and churches harmoniously surround every square, and where statues stand in silent watch over gardens and parks.

Declared a Unesco World Heritage Site, the city centre has been unmarred by the building boom that has taken over the rest of post-Soviet Russia. But it's not a museum-city. It's a lively metropolis, filled with clubs, restaurants, theatres and music, with a large population of students and young people, and more cars and hustle than the city can sometimes manage.

The Northern Capital

For a young city, St Petersburg has had a rich and turbulent history. The home of the Russian court for over 200 years, its palaces were the sites of royal triumphs and sorrows – and not a few assassinations. It was the home of the arts, the city that reinvented ballet, that inspired the best of Russia's poets and writers, and that became home to some of the finest art in the world. But it was also the city that brought down the Romanov dynasty and became the 'cradle of the revolution'. Its streets and museums are filled with the memories of those first years of revolution and the Soviet era. It

The magnificent Winter Palace

Symbols of the city

The crest of St Petersburg, approved by Empress Anna in 1730, is based on its role as a port city: two anchors crossed under a sceptre topped by the double-headed eagle of Russia. But three other symbols are frequently used for the city: the ship weathervane at the top of the Admiralty spire, the angel atop the Cathedral of St Peter and Paul, and the Bronze Horseman, Falconet's brilliant statue of Peter the Great in Decembrist Square.

is also the Hero City of Leningrad that withstood the German army's 900-day blockade during World War II, what Russians call the 'Great Patriotic War'.

In the Soviet period, St Petersburg suffered the rather benign neglect of its leaders. On the one hand, they didn't subject it to the kind of reconstruction that completely transformed Moscow; on the other hand, they barely invested in the city's upkeep. By the end of the Soviet era and in the first years of the new Russian Federation, St Petersburg became a rather run-down, dirty and dowdy city. Even the gilding had faded on the cupolas and spires.

But under the energetic rule of Governor Valentina Matvienko, the city has been reclaiming its birthright. And for the 300th anniversary of the city in 2003 and G-8 meetings in 2006, St Petersburg received an influx of funding that has begun to transform the city.

21st-Century City

St Petersburg is a city for art-lovers. It is filled with the glories of pre-revolutionary architecture and civic art, and has the best art collections in Russia; the Hermitage is one of the world's largest and most dazzling museums, second only to the Louvre in the number and quality of its masterpieces. And that is only one museum in this museum-filled city. It rivals Moscow in its performing arts, particularly the Kirov ballet, which has preserved and developed the finest traditions of Russian dance. And if you get tired of urban beauty, you can go out to the 'necklace' of palace estates that encircle the city: the grand blue-and-gold Catherine Palace at Tsarskoe Selo; the more intimate palace of Pavlovsk, nestled in a beautifully landscaped park; or Peterhof, the Russian Versailles, with a breathtaking Grand Palace and parks dotted with hundreds of fountains, including the golden masterpiece of the Grand Cascade.

In the past few years St Petersburg has become very tourist-friendly, with more signs in English, shops catering to tourists, and a range of hotels and 'mini-hotels'. Thousands of restaurants and cafés offer every kind of cuisine, including wonderfully updated and innovative Russian classics. Clubs and bars get jumping nearly every night, and you can enjoy everything from folk concerts to jazz to reggae.

A sunny day in the city

The city seems rather small, but this is deceptive: almost 5 million people live in St Petersburg, most of them in housing estates far from the city centre, but connected by public transport. It is a fairly homogeneous population – the vast majority of the residents are Slavs, with smaller populations from the former Soviet republics. People tend to be well dressed in the European manner, and there is still a bit of aristocratic gentility in native residents.

The ice on the Neva begins to break up in spring

When to Go

St Petersburg is only six degrees south of the Arctic Circle and the most northern city in the world with a population of over 1 million people. Although the sea mitigates the climate, which averages about 20°C (68°F) in the summer and -5°C (23°F) in the winter, the damp can be piercing, and the wind off the Gulf of Finland is wicked. Since it is so far north, the city enjoys the magnificent White Nights in high summer: from mid-June to mid-July, the sky barely darkens at night, and the city is filled with strollers and revellers 24 hours a day. But in the winter, residents and visitors pay for the glorious summer sun with only a few hours of pallid sunlight a day.

The best time to visit is during the summer, when the city never sleeps and all the city's palaces, parks and fountains are open to the public – and when there are arts festivals virtually every week. But it is also beautiful in deep winter, when snow lies on the gold spires and cupolas, the city seems nestled in a white down, and the ice on the rivers and canals glimmers in the weak sun. 'Golden autumn' is a great time for performing-arts-lovers who want to enjoy the season's premières.

Late spring is also a good time for a visit – before the tourist crowds (and price rises), but with mild weather and the arts in full swing. Only the early spring doesn't show the city off at its best, particularly April, when the parks and gardens are closed to dry after the winter. But even then, the celebration of Maslenitsa (Pancake Week) before Lent brings a festive air to the city. And there is nothing like watching – and hearing – the ice break up on the Neva: it seems to moan before finally cracking under the onslaught of spring.

In Transition

Petersburgers lament that they have an imperial city with a provincial budget. Although there is a great deal of industrial production in and around the city, Moscow has had the biggest share of the petro-dollars that are fuelling the country's economic revival. The city is still in transition. The buildings on smaller lanes have yet to get a new coat of paint, shops are plentiful but shopping isn't yet like Paris or London, and some of the older museums have a dusty smell and old-fashioned exhibits.

Young sailors on the *Aurora*

But that is also the city's charm: corners of St Petersburg are still untouched by time and let you seamlessly drift into the past, to centuries without cars and lifts and neon. After a few days in St Petersburg, you are sure to fall under the city's spell.

A BRIEF HISTORY

St Petersburg's history is brief – just over 300 years. Yet in that time a magnificent city rose out of the marshland, was nearly destroyed by invading armies, plundered by its own people, and then slipped into provincial decline – only to rise once again as a great centre of art, beauty and culture.

Russia Before Peter the Great

The Russian empire grew slowly from the 9th century. The successor state to Kievan Rus, Russia was first a jumble of city-states ruled by Grand Princes. Attacked by the Tatars (called Mongols in the West) in the 13th century and kept under their rule for nearly 250 years, the state developed without real contact with European powers. After vanquishing the 'Tatar-Mongol Yoke', Moscow began to gather many of its neighbouring city-states into its sphere. This new state of Russia was tightly connected with the Russian Orthodox Church, which considered itself the successor to the 'fallen Church' of Rome and Constantinople.

Russian Orthodox icon

Following a period of chaos called the Time of Troubles after the original ruling house came to an end, a new dynasty appeared in 1613 when Mikhail Romanov took the crown. Russia under the first Romanovs had a prosperous and grand capital in Moscow and was more Eastern than Western in appearance, outlook and habit.

Peter's City

Then came the Romanov who would be called Peter the Great. Traumatised by a rebellion that took the lives of his family, Peter largely grew up on the outskirts of the capital. A huge man (2m/ 6ft 7in tall) with enormous energy, curiosity and a keen mind, he set off to Europe incognito to study the crafts, arts, sciences and state institutions of his European neighbours. After putting down several rebellions, he crowned himself emperor and began a series of reforms to bring Russia into European civilisation.

In 1700 he declared war on Sweden, which at the time controlled the majority of the Baltic Sea region. By 1703 Russia had taken the entire length of the Neva river, and Peter founded a new port,

Peter's foundations

According to legend, when the foundation was being laid for the Peter and Paul Fortress, an eagle soared in the sky, a sign of divine approbation.

which he called Sankt Pieter Burkh in the Dutch manner after his patron saint. Peter envisioned a totally planned city, with streets laid out in a regular grid and civic architecture designed around squares and gardens. It was to be a rational, Western city – the opposite of Eastern Moscow, with its streets scattered willy-nilly around the Kremlin fortress in the centre. The conditions during construction were appalling: perhaps up to

100,000 workers died of fever and disease in the marshy land. The Russian court baulked at moving to this wilderness, but Peter insisted, and in 1712 he forced 1,000 noble families and 500 merchant families to move north. By the time of Peter's death in 1725 the city's population had risen to 40,000.

The Age of the Empresses

After Peter's death, his wife Catherine and then grandson Peter rebelled and moved the court back to Moscow. But Empress Anna (reigned 1730–40) returned the court to St Petersburg, hired Bartolomeo Rastrelli as court architect and began to commission the city's magnificent Russian baroque palaces. Anna and her successor, the Empress Elizabeth (reigned 1741–62) were great lovers of balls and beauty. Under Elizabeth, the Winter Palace, Smolny Convent and Catherine Palace were begun, and Peterhof was redesigned.

Anna's Ice Palace

During the early years of the St Petersburg court, emperors and empresses had 'court jokers' – usually noblemen who had displeased the ruler or defied the law. During the reign of Empress Anna, Prince Mikhail Golitsyn married an Italian woman and converted to Catholicism. The enraged empress annulled the marriage and designated the prince as one of her court jokers. For a laugh, she decided to marry her Kalmyk maid to the prince and build a honeymoon palace for them on the Neva river by the Winter Palace. Over 17m (56ft) long and 5m (16.5ft) wide, this palace made of carved blocks of ice and everything inside was also ice: furniture, clocks, flowers in vases and even cards laid out on an ice table – all lit by thousands of candles in ice candlesticks. The poor couple somehow survived their wedding night in the palace, which stood on the frozen river all February and March of 1740. A copy of the palace was carved out of ice on Palace Square in 2006, although no one was forced – or allowed – to spend the night.

The second Catherine became known as Catherine the Great (1762–96). The German wife of Peter III, she ended her husband's brief rule with a coup and assumed the throne. She was both famously liberal, corresponding with Voltaire and instituting some key reforms, and famously imperious and imperial, fighting down a peasant rebellion and enlarging the Russian empire. Her building spree in the capital introduced neoclassicism to the city, and she

Catherine the Great

built the Little and Old Hermitages, the Hermitage Theatre and the Marble Palace, as well as the Bronze Horseman, the statue of Peter the Great. Under the reign of these empresses, St Petersburg ceased to be an oasis of luxury in the wilderness and began to be the grand capital that Peter had envisioned.

Stumbling towards Reform

When Catherine died, her son Paul ruled briefly (1796–1801) before being killed in his bed in a palace coup. His son Alexander came to the throne. The entire 19th century was ruled by tsars named Alexander and Nicholas, who moved towards and away from modern democratic institutions. Each built new palaces and cathedrals, squares and monuments, bringing their own style and vision to Peter's city. By the end of the century, St Petersburg was a vibrant city, filled with artists, poets, writers, scientists and scholars, as well as a growing population of merchants and industrialists – and a vast population of artisans and working people.

View of the Strelka when it was the city's port

Alexander I (reigned 1801–25) began as a moderate reformer, but became more conservative over the course of his reign. Russia under this tsar was attacked by French armies led by Napoleon, who captured the Kremlin before being forced into retreat. During the first Alexander's reign, the General Staff Building and the Alexander Column, erected in honour of the hard-won victory over Napoleon, completed the architectural ensemble of Palace Square. Alexander I also had the Strelka redesigned, with a new Stock Exchange building and the landmark Rostral Columns.

The reign (1825–55) of his brother Nicholas I is remembered for the Decembrist uprising – a group of noblemen who called for a constitution and were executed or exiled for their heresy. Nicholas I had his favourite architect, Carlo Rossi, design the buildings of the Senate and Alexandrinskaya ploshchad (now Ostrovskovo), one of the most aesthetically pleasing squares in the city. Nicholas also had the first railroad built (in 1837, between the city and Tsarskoe Selo) and the first permanent bridge over the Neva.

Alexander II (1855–81) was the 'Tsar Liberator' who freed the serfs and instituted a number of important reforms. But the emancipation of the serfs and nascent industrialisation brought thousands of the poor into the city. Tenements went up to house them, and grander apartment buildings appeared for the growing middle class. The arts flourished, but the social inequities seemed to grow worse. This enlightened tsar might have responded to stem the tide of rebellion, but was, ironically, killed by an assassin's bomb.

His son, Alexander III (reigned 1881–94) did not rule long, and his time at the helm of state was reactionary and conservative. When he died suddenly in 1894, his son Nicholas II found himself on the throne: a kind and pious man utterly unprepared for the role history had thrust on him. In 1904 the 'short, victorious war' with Japan that he attempted to arrange ended with the destruction of the Russian navy, then in 1905 he was implicated in the massacre of peaceful demonstrators on 'Bloody Sunday'. All the while he struggled with his own family tragedy of an ailing heir *(see box right)*. He blundered into the new century, doing nothing to stop the unrest and seemingly doing everything to make it worse.

Grigory Rasputin

When Nicholas II's son and heir, Alexei, was discovered to suffer from haemophilia, the desperate Empress Alexandra turned to Grigory Rasputin, a debauched Siberian peasant who claimed to be a mystical healer. Somehow he managed to ease the Tsarevich's suffering, and Alexandra fell under his spell. One of the tsar's advisers wrote: 'His wife ruled the state and Rasputin ruled her. Rasputin inspired, the empress ordered, the tsar obeyed.' Rasputin was eventually killed by a group of noblemen in 1916.

What's in a name?

In August 1914, with Russia at war with Germany, Nicholas II ordered the city name changed to the Russian Petrograd (*grad* is the old Russian word for city). Three days after Vladimir Lenin's death in 1924, the name was changed to Leningrad. In 1991 the residents voted to restore the city's original name, although when the war years are remembered, Leningrad is often used in memory of those who died under that name. Among residents the city is simply called 'Peter'.

While the empire seemed to slide towards collapse, the city continued to grow, especially with *style moderne* (Art Nouveau) mansions and apartment buildings that blended perfectly with the baroque and classical legacy.

The Revolution

When Russia entered World War I in 1914 and suffered enormous losses, the poverty-stricken, weary and deprived population had reached the end of its patience. In March 1917 the last tsar, Nicholas II, abdicated and was succeeded by a Provisional Government. Vladimir Lenin, a professional revolutionary, saw his chance to exploit the chaos and discontent. He and his comrades arrived at Finland Station in April 1917 and made brief rousing remarks to a crowd of workers that had been rallied at the station.

Lenin and his Bolsheviks jockeyed for power in the workers' soviets (councils) that countered the Provisional Government. On the night of 25 October 1917 they set in motion a coup d'état. The battleship *Aurora* fired a blank shot that signalled the start of the coup. Their soldiers claimed the city's strategic railway stations, post office, banks and bridges, and then finally escorted the Provisional Government out of the Winter Palace. Few shots were fired. At first the rest of the country had little idea that anything had happened at all.

The Bolshevik hold on power was not absolute at first, and they moved the capital to Moscow in 1918 to ensure greater safety. The coup turned into a civil war, which lasted until 1922. St Petersburg's first year of Soviet power was marked by bitter poverty, famine and violence, first born of chaos and then used as a tool of state repression. The tsar, his family and relatives were killed in 1918. Private housing was turned into communal apartments; palaces and mansions were claimed as state offices or turned into museums; churches were torn down or made into dormitories, warehouses or offices. The population fled: in 1915 the city had over 2 million inhabitants; by 1920 there were less than 800,000.

The city of the arts began to lose its geniuses. The artistic elite emigrated, died of hunger, and then were silenced by the censors or worse – sent to prison, exile or the executioner. Economically the city began to revive somewhat in the 1930s, when Stalin began his great industrialisation effort and decided to move the centre of the city south, starting work on the

Painting of the revolution in the Artillery Museum

Much of St Petersburg was destroyed during World War II

enormous House of Soviets that was to be the heart of Leningrad. But economic revival was accompanied by purges of the Party, military and industrial elite in waves of campaigns to rid the country of 'anti-Soviet elements'. While figures are still debated, it is certain that at least 1 million people were killed in the repressions, including the top military leaders.

World War II

The loss of the army's best leaders was one reason the country was unprepared for Hitler's forces when they attacked on 22 June 1941. The Nazi armies quickly moved through the west of the country and arrived at the outskirts of Leningrad by September. Most of the treasures in the city's museums were packed and shipped east by train, and whatever could not be removed was buried underground or hidden by netting and camouflage. For 900 days, from 8 September 1941 to 27 January 1944, the Germans blockaded and relentlessly bombed the city.

Secret documents discovered after the war showed the Wehrmacht's intention to destroy the population. One read: 'The Führer is determined to eliminate the city of Petersburg from the face of earth.' Hitler planned to celebrate New Year 1942 in the imperial palaces and even printed invitations to a reception at the Astoria Hotel. During that winter the constant bombing destroyed the already scant food supplies, and rations were decreased to 400g/15oz of bread for a worker and 200g/7.5oz for a woman or child. As the winter continued, rations were reduced further still, to 250g/9oz and 125g/4.5oz respectively.

Some relief came with the opening of the Road of Life across the frozen Lake Ladoga, but supplies only resumed when the blockade was broken in 1944. By then much of the city had been destroyed, virtually all of the suburban palaces had been plundered, burned and blown up. Over 1 million people died, but the German armies never entered the city.

Collapse of the Soviet Union

The city rebuilt after the war, but throughout the late Soviet period, it had a rather odd status: a cultural capital equal to Moscow with services at the level of provincial Tula. Perhaps it is no wonder that when Mikhail Gorbachev came to power in 1985 and introduced his policies of glasnost (openness) and perestroika (restructuring) – designed to help the nation to face up to its backwardness and revamp its moribund economy – St Petersburg became one of the strongest centres pushing for reform.

When a group of hardliners in the Soviet government organised a coup in August 1991, the leadership and population of the city were determined to defend their rights. The Kirov factory provided fax communications with the centre of resistance led by Boris Yeltsin in Moscow, Mayor Anatoly Sobchak defied the State Emergency Committee (the coup

Russian dolls

organisers) on local television, taxi drivers used their radios to pass on information about possible troop movements, and nearly 200,000 people streamed into Palace Square. No troops entered the city. By the end of three tense days, the city and nation had left their Soviet past behind. At the end of 1991 the Soviet Union was disbanded and the Russian Federation tricolour flag appeared on the city's spires for the first time in over 70 years.

The city, like the country as a whole, suffered greatly in the economic upheavals of the 1990s, as the leaders struggled to dismantle the old system and lay the foundations for capitalism – while fighting the old guard eager to turn back the clock. Hyperinflation, devaluation of the rouble and the default on government loans in 1998 wiped out people's savings. The absence of a modern legal and banking system thwarted the growth of new businesses. St Petersburg did not reap immediate economic benefits from post-Soviet economic change; indeed, it got more gangsters than businessmen, and its beautiful palaces and museums became run-down and derelict.

The city finally got a break in 2000, when Vladimir Putin came to power after Boris Yeltsin resigned. A native of the city, Putin began to shower it with funds. Increased foreign and domestic investment and plans to move the Constitutional Court to the city's former Senate buildings have been helping St Petersburg repair a century of damage and bring new life, business and art to the northern capital.

Historical Landmarks

1703 Peter the Great founds the city.

1712 The imperial court is moved to the city.

1725 Catherine I moves the capital back to Moscow after Peter's death.

1730 Empress Anna returns the capital to St Petersburg.

1754 Rastrelli begins the Winter Palace.

1757 The Academy of Arts is founded.

1762 Catherine II (the Great) begins her reign.

1801 Catherine II's son Paul is murdered and Alexander I takes the throne.

1812 Napoleon's armies attack Russia and capture the Kremlin.

1818 St Isaac's Cathedral is begun.

1825 The Decembrist rebellion.

1851 The rail line opens between Moscow and St Petersburg.

1855 Alexander II assumes the throne.

1858 St Isaac's Cathedral is completed.

1861 The emancipation of the serfs.

1881 Alexander II is assassinated and Alexander III assumes the throne.

1894 Nicholas II assumes the throne.

1904–5 Russo-Japanese War.

1913 300th Anniversary of the Romanov dynasty.

1914 Russia enters World War I and the city is renamed Petrograd.

1917 In February the tsar abdicates; in October the Bolsheviks stage a coup against the Provisional Government.

1918 Capital moved to Moscow; imperial family killed in Yekaterinburg.

1922 Civil war ends with the formation of the USSR.

1924 Lenin dies and the city is renamed Leningrad.

1941–4 900-day blockade of Leningrad during World War II.

1991 The USSR is dissolved and the city is renamed St Petersburg.

1999 Boris Yeltsin, first president of Russia, resigns on 31 December.

2000 Vladimir Putin, son of St Petersburg, elected president.

2003 The city celebrates its 300th anniversary.

2007 Dozens detained as riot police break up protest accusing Putin of stifling democracy.

WHERE TO GO

Although St Petersburg is a sprawling metropolis with a population of almost 5 million, the historical centre is fairly compact. The city is bisected by the Neva river, which splits into the Bolshaya (Great) and Malaya (Small) Neva at its widest point near the Spit and Hare Island. Although canals and rivers snake through the city, the streets are laid out in a grid, with the central street of Nevsky prospekt cutting through the city, and squares and parks at major intersections. For the purposes of this guide, we have divided the city into six geographically distinct sections. A final section describes some of the palaces in the 'necklace' of suburban estates that rings the city.

St Petersburg's grid plan and well-marked streets make it easy to navigate on foot. To get from one end of Nevsky prospekt to the other, you can jump on one of the buses or trolleys that ply the main street, and to get across town, it's easy to hop on the efficient metro. For a trip out of the city, there are tour buses every day, or freelance guides with drivers. In the summer months, the most enjoyable way to get to Peterhof is by hydrofoil along the Neva.

St Petersburg's huge art and historical museums can seem daunting to visitors with just a few days in the city. The Hermitage likes to tell visitors that it would take 15 years of daily eight-hour visits to spend just a minute on each of the treasures in its vast collection – and that's just one museum in this museum-laden city. Unless money is a concern, the best way to see the Hermitage and other museums is in small increments each day, with breaks for shopping, a bite to eat, and the other pleasures of the city.

The Admiralty

PETROGRAD SIDE

The Petrograd Side (Петро-
градская сторона – Petro-
gradskaya storona) encom-
passes three main islands,
including **Hare Island**
(Заячий остров – Zayachy
ostrov), the small island
where the city began, **Petrograd Island** (Петроградский
остров – Petgrogradsky ostrov) and **Aptekarsky Island**
(Аптекарский остров). Peter
laid the foundations for the
Peter and Paul Fortress here,

The Romanov family crest

and the islands were largely populated by workers, artisans
and merchants, until the Trinity Bridge over the Neva was
completed in 1903. The building boom on the Petrograd Side
coincided with the passion for *style moderne* (Art Nouveau)
architecture, and the island is considered to have the best and
most numerous examples of this style in the city, especially
along Kamennoostrovsky prospekt. Most of the sights are a
comfortable walk from the city's beginnings in the Peter and
Paul Fortress on the banks of the Neva.

Peter and Paul Fortress

➤ **Peter and Paul Fortress** (Петропавловская крепость –
Petropavlovskaya krepost; open Tue 11am–4pm, Thur–Mon
11am–6pm, closed last Tue of the month; admission fee),
where the city began, was originally built of wood and called
Sankt Pieter Burkh in honour of the Apostle St Peter. Although it was built to withstand an attack from the Swedes,
its battlements were never tested. Over the centuries its struc-

tures have served as a prison, a mint, the resting place of the imperial family, and the first rocket-engine laboratory (in the 1930s). Today it is part of the Museum of St Petersburg's History *(see pages 61–2)*, and despite its rather dark past, it is a fascinating place, with one of Russia's most beautiful cathedrals and a number of museums that give an excellent introduction to the history of the city.

The stone walls of the fortress, built in 1706–40 by Domenico Trezzini, have six bastions named after Peter the Great's closest companions: the Gosuradev (the sovereign), Menshikov, Golovkin, Zotov, Trubetskoy and Naryshkin. The main entrance, at the northwest corner, is through two gates: the rather plain **Ivan's Gate** (Иоанновские ворота – Ioannovskie vorota), built in 1730, and the lavish **Peter's Gate** (Петровские ворота – Petrovskie vorota), built in 1717–18 by Trezzini. Above the Peter's Gate portal is the two-headed eagle and a bas-relief carved by Conradt Osner for the first wooden gate. It depicts the Apostle Peter casting down Simon Magus – a symbol of Peter's victory over the Swedes. On either side of the portal are niches with statues of Bellona, the Roman goddess of war, and Minerva, the goddess of wisdom and crafts.

Peter and Paul Cathedral glistens behind the battlements

The main gate to the river, the **Neva Gate** (Невские ворота – Nevskie vorota), was built in 1730–1 and redesigned to its present austere classical appearance in 1787. To the west of the gate is a narrow strip of land between the fortress and water which is covered with sunbathers in good weather. In the winter, human 'walruses' break the ice for a quick dip in the frigid water.

Peter and Paul Cathedral

The fortress originally had a small wooden chapel dedicated to Sts Peter and Paul, but when Peter the Great moved the capital here in 1712, he commissioned Trezzini to build the **Peter and Paul Cathedral** (Петропавловский собор – Petropavlovsky sobor), which would be Russia's main house of worship. Legend has it that Peter took part in the design himself, insisting on the architectural innovation of an enormous spire covered in gold. The height of the cathedral is 122½m (402ft), of which 30m (98ft) is the spire itself. Originally made of gilded wood, after several fires it was finally changed to steel in 1857–8.

The interior of the cathedral was also an innovation: instead of the traditional Russian Orthodox cross plan,

The baroque interior of the Peter and Paul Cathedral

it is built in the style of West-ern churches: a long rectangle divided into three naves by enormous pilasters. It is a magnificent example of early baroque architecture: pale-green and rose pilasters, glittering chandeliers, and a many-tiered carved and gild-ed wooden iconostasis remi-niscent of a triumphal arch

Laying Peter to rest

Peter the Great did not live to see his cathedral com-pleted; he died in 1725 and was interred in a wooden chapel inside the cathedral. When the cathedral was completed in 1733 and consecrated, he was placed in the church's first crypt.

with 43 icons. The cathedral is the resting place of all the tsars after Peter the Great, with the exception of Peter II, who is in-terred in the Kremlin. In 1998, after lengthy forensic investi-gations, remains unearthed outside of Yekaterinburg were determined to be the imperial family, and Nicholas II, Alexan-dra and three daughters were interred here.

Next to the cathedral is the **Mausoleum of the Grand Dukes** (Великокняжеская усыпальница – Velikoknyazh-eskaya usypalnitsa), built in 1896–1906 by the architect David Grimm, where 60 members of the imperial family are interred. Nearby is the **Boat House** (Ботный дом – Botny dom), where Peter the Great's first boat was orig-inally displayed (now found in the Central Navy Museum, *see page 35*).

The fortress was used as a prison even as it was being built: Peter the Great incarcerated his son Alexei, whom he accused of treason, in the 'Secret House' here in 1718, where he was tortured to death (possibly with the tsar's par-ticipation). Before the house was demolished, the Decem-brists *(see page 16)* were also held here before execution, as was writer Fyodor Dostoevsky. In 1872 the **Trubetskoy Bastion** was turned into a prison, where an illustrious group of political prisoners were held, including the ministers of

Shemyakin's statue

Near the cathedral is the avant-garde artist Mikhail Shemyakin's statue of Peter the Great, placed in 1991. The odd sculpture, with its disproportioned head and hands, scandalised city residents when it was installed. But now it seems to be accepted: people rub the right index finger for good luck.

the tsar and members of the imperial family and Provisional Government. It was turned into a museum in 1924. Visitors can see cells, punishment rooms and the guard room, as well as an exhibition of photographs and other artefacts from the history of the prison.

The two-floored **Commandant's House** (1743–6) and the **Engineer's House** (1748–9) display temporary and permanent exhibitions about the history of the city.

Kronverk and the Embankment

Fearing attacks from the fortress's vulnerable land side to the north, Peter the Great had a series of earthen battlements, ditches, a moat and weaponry installed in what is called **Kronverk** (Кронверк) because the shape of the area looked like a crown. In the 19th century it was the site of the execution of Decembrists, and then used to house the arsenal. The horseshoe-shaped brick building was designed by Pyotr Tamansky in 1849–60. Today it is the **Artillery Museum** (Военно-исторический музей артиллерии – Voenno-istorichesky muzey artillerii; Alexandrovsky Park 7; open Wed–Sun 11am–6pm; admission fee) which displays every kind of weapon used in Russia, along with tanks, banners, flags, uniforms and other military equipment.

Behind the Artillery Museum is the **Alexandrovsky Park**, a stretch of land that was originally left empty so that enemies could be easily spied creeping up on the fortress. In the mid-19th century it was turned into a park, and until the revolution offered a combination of genteel and rowdy pleasures, from an opera house to the zoo. Today it has cafés, casinos, a zoo *(see page 94)*, an amusement park and a planetarium (open Tue–Sun 10.30am–6pm).

Near the entrance to the Peter and Paul Fortress is **Trinity Square**, once the site of a cathedral and the first Stock Exchange, and the bustling centre of life on the island. Nearby is the **Museum of Political History** (Музей политической истории – Muzey politicheskoy istorii; ulitsa Kuybisheva 2/4; open Fri–Wed 10am–6pm; admission fee), housed in two now united *style moderne* mansions owned by the ballerina Matilda Kshesynskaya and Baron Brandt. Kshesynskaya's house was commandeered by Lenin and his cohorts in 1917 and now displays Lenin's preserved study, photographs, posters and other political memorabilia, and includes constantly running videos from virtually every era as well as tapes of the leaders' speeches. Several rooms recreate life in the Kshesynskaya mansion when the prima ballerina lived there.

Stained-glass windows at the Museum of Political History

On the bank of the Neva stands the little house that Peter the Great first lived in when he began to build his city. The log **Cabin of Peter the Great** (Домик Петра – Domik Petra; Petrovskaya nab. 6; open Wed–Mon 10am–5.30pm, closed last Mon of the month; admission fee) was built 24–26 May 1703 and is the only wooden structure from the Petrine period to survive to this day. In 1844, it was surrounded by a brick shell to protect it from St Petersburg's destructive climate. Inside are the rustic little rooms where this giant of a tsar lived until 1708 whenever he was in the city.

A bit further down on the embankment is the famous **Cruiser Aurora** (Крейсер Аврора – Kreyser Avrora, Petrovskaya nab.; open Tue–Thur and Sat–Sun 10.30am–4pm; admission fee) that fired the blank shot to signal the attack on the Winter Palace in 1917. The ship was built in 1900 and served in the ill-fated Russo-Japanese War before being turned into a training vessel. Today the ship's crew quarters, machinery and famous weaponry are all open to visitors, along with lots of revolutionary memorabilia.

The imposing Cruiser *Aurora*

If you want to know what life was like in the early Soviet period, visit the apartment where Sergey Kirov, the head of the city's Party administration lived in 1926–34. The **Kirov Museum** (Музей С.М. Кирова – Muzey S.M. Kirova; Kamennoostrovsky prospekt 26/28; open Thur–Tue 11am–5.30pm; admission fee) is a bit like walking back in time, since everything – bedroom slippers, books, hunting trophies, art – is intact, as is his office taken from the Party headquarters. There are exhibits of photographs and memorabilia from his life and mysterious death, as well as a fascinating and detailed exhibition on childhood during the Stalinist era that recreates settings from children's life in the 1920s and 1930s.

Sergey Kirov

Sergey Kirov (1886–1934) was a leading revolutionary who headed St Petersburg's Party organisation and city administration from 1926 until his death. A good manager, charismatic speaker and popular leader, he was a close friend of Joseph Stalin. In 1934 he was shot in the back of the head as he entered his office in the Smolny Institute. Historians believe that his death was ordered by Stalin as a pretext for launching his Great Purges.

Kirov Islands

The **Kirov Islands** (Кировские острова–Kirovskie ostrova), to the northeast of Petrograd Side, are three pretty havens from urban life. **Kamenny** is rapidly becoming a gated community for the rich and famous; **Krestovsky** is dominated by the large Victory Park, and **Yelagin** is home to a lovely park and **Yelagin Palace** (open Wed–Sun 10am–6pm; admission fee), a neoclassical mansion built in 1818–22 by Carlo Rossi for Alexander I's mother. The primary joy of all three islands is nature: paths winding through woods and along river banks are filled with families and friends enjoying a break from the city.

Vasilevsky Island at sunset

VASILEVSKY ISLAND

Peter the Great originally planned for Vasilevsky Island
(Васильевский остров – Vasilevsky ostrov) to be the administrative centre of his new city, with canals cut in straight lines
across the island. He built several administrative buildings,
but flooding and lack of access from the southern side of the
river (and the road to Moscow) put an end to his plans. Many
of his administration buildings are now educational institutions or museums, and the intended canals are city streets with
the unusual name of 'lines'. Most of the attractions are near
the Strelka (Spit), but Bolshoy prospekt and the quiet, largely residential 'lines' are pleasant for strolls.

Strelka
The Spit (Стрелка – Strelka) is a triangle of land that juts
out where the Neva divides into the Bolshaya and Malaya

Neva rivers. The present architecture was designed by Thomas de Thomon and Andreyan Zakharov in 1810: the monumental Stock Exchange flanked by two warehouses overlooking a small park with two mighty lighthouses. The lighthouses, called the **Rostral Columns** (Ростральные колонны – Rostralnye kolonny, from the Latin *rostra*, a stage in Rome decorated with the prows of captured ships), are 32m (105ft) high and decorated with allegorical images of Russia's four great rivers: the Neva, Volga, Dnieper and Volkhov. They were originally lit with oil lamps as navigational lights.

The classical Stock Exchange is now the **Central Navy Museum** (Центральный Военно-морской музей – Tsentralny Voenno-morskoy muzey; Birzhevaya ploshchad 4; open Wed–Sun 10.30am–5.30pm, closed last Thur of the month; admission fee), crammed full of every kind of ship and nautical device, including Peter the Great's original 'little boat' that he learned to sail in, and a particularly rich collection of Soviet posters, flags, naval and political memorabilia.

The north warehouse that flanked the Stock Exchange now houses two institutes; next to it is the former Customs House, now the Institute of Russian Literature. The south warehouse houses the **Zoological Museum** (Зоологический музей – Zoologichesky muzey; Universitetskaya nab. 1/3; open Sat–Thur 11am–6pm; admission fee), filled with thousands of stuffed creatures of land, air and sea, including some baby mammoths dating back over 40,000 years.

Rostral Column detail

University Embankment

Next to the Zoological Museum on the embankment is the **Museum of Anthropology and Ethnography and Kunst-kamera** (Музей антропологии и этнографии, Кунсткамера – Muzey antropologii i etnographii, Kunstkamera; Universitetskaya nab. 3; open Tue–Sun daily 11am–5pm, closed last Tue of the month; admission fee), a marvellous Petrine baroque structure built 1718–34 by Georg Johann Mattarnovy to house Peter the Great's Cabinet of Curiosities. Peter I bought them from the Dutch scientist Frederik Ruysch in 1717, and put them on display to dispel his people's superstitions. He wanted them to see that physical abnormalities were natural phenomena and not the work of witches or the devil. The collection of anatomical oddities is displayed in the rotunda to packed crowds of adults and children, although the collection may be disturbing to some visitors.

The Twelve Colleges

The museum also has an extensive and truly wonderful collection of apparel and ethnographic artefacts from all over the world. In the circular hall of the tower is the study where Mikhail Lomonosov, Russia's first and most prominent scientist and scholar, worked in 1741–65, and the spectacular **Great Gottorp Globe**, which requires a separate ticket to see. The current globe replaced the original presented to Peter the Great in 1713, which was destroyed by fire. Over 3m (9ft) in diameter, it shows the world on the outside and the heavens on the inside.

Further west along the embankment of the Bolshaya Neva is the spectacular red-and-white Petrine baroque building of the **Twelve Colleges** (Двенадцать коллегий – Dvenadtsat kollegy), built in 1743 by Domenico Trezzini and stretching over 400m (1,300ft) perpendicular to the river bank. Originally meant for Peter the Great's 'collegium' of ministers, it became part of the university in the 19th century. The entire embankment and neighbourhood is the heart of St Petersburg's academic world, with students and professors dodging tourists on their way to classes.

Nearby is the **Menshikov Palace** (Дворец Меншикова – Dvorets Menshikova; Universitetskaya nab. 15; open Tue–Sun 10.30am–5pm; admission fee), the first stone building in the city, built in 1710–27 by a number of architects including Domenico Trezzini, Bartolomeo Rastrelli and Jean-Baptiste Le Blond. Built for Peter the Great's best friend and companion, Prince Alexander Menshikov, whom the sovereign appointed first governor of St Petersburg, the palace served as the official site for foreign receptions and unofficial carousing by Peter and his friends. Restored to its original appearance in 2002, it is a magnificent Petrine Dutch-inspired residence, with halls on a human scale, from the

Peter's pal

Alexander Menshikov (1673–1729) was Peter the Great's best friend and companion. Of lowly background, Menshikov had the intelligence and military and administrative skill to win the tsar's favour, and apparently enough charm for the tsar to forgive his greed, embezzling and corrupt practices. After Peter's death, he was stripped of his titles and wealth, and banished to Siberia, where he died.

Egyptian sphinxes

On the embankment in front of the Academy of Arts are 14th-century BC sphinxes brought to St Petersburg in 1832.

kitchens to the reception rooms decorated by tapestries and silk wallpaper, to the private quarters entirely tiled from floor to ceiling.

Further west is the **Academy of Arts** (Академия Художеств – Akademiya khudozhestv; Universitetskaya nab. 17; open Wed–Sun 11am–6pm; admission fee), founded in 1757 by the Empress Elizabeth and built by Alexander Kokorinov and Vallin de la Mothe. The imposing neoclassical building has a rather dusty, old-fashioned ambience, with earnest students practising their drawing in the halls of the museum. Most of the Academy's best works were distributed to other museums after the 1917 revolution, but the collection of academic paintings and drawings is worth a look. Be sure to troop up to the top floor to see the architectural scale models of some of the city's most famous structures, including several versions of the Smolny Convent and St Isaac's Cathedral.

THE PALACE EMBANKMENT

It's a rare visitor to St Petersburg who doesn't gasp in awe at the first glimpse of enormous Palace Square and Winter Palace. This is the heart and soul of the city, with one of the world's greatest art museums, the Hermitage.

There were three small palaces on this side of the river before Empress Anna commissioned Bartolomeo Rastrelli to build a proper Winter Palace (Зимний дворец – Zimny dvorets) in 1754. Empress Elizabeth wasn't entirely satisfied with Anna's palace and had Rastrelli redo the residence. What you see now was completed in 1762, although parts were reconstructed after a devastating fire in 1837 or slightly modified over the years. The pale minty-blue walls, gold decoration and syncopated columns give the enormous, 1,057-room winter residence of the tsars a lightness that belies its massive size.

Catherine the Great had most of the interiors redecorated in her favourite neoclassical style, but she didn't alter the exteriors and some of Rastrelli's most magnificent halls. But she did make one enormous change: Although her predecessors had collected art, Catherine was a fanatic, and she built the Little Hermitage and Large Hermitage to hold

The Winter Palace at sunset

Quite a collection

Russian emperors and empresses filled their collection by purchasing large foreign collections, including those once owned by Robert Walpole, John Lyde-Brown, the Empress Josephine, Cristoforo Barbarigo and Gian Pietro Campana.

her growing collection, and then built the theatre to enjoy other artistic pleasures. Nicholas I, another serious collector, commissioned the New Hermitage and in 1852 opened part of the collection to the public as the Imperial Museum, with an entryway guarded by 10 magnificent 5m (16ft) Atlases (male figures decoratively supporting a building). Today the entire complex of imperial residence and art museum is housed in these five interconnected buildings on the embankment.

In 1917 after the abdication of the tsar, the Provisional Government took up residence in the Winter Palace. On 25 October 1917 the palace was attacked by Bolsheviks, although the palace was not 'stormed' by thousands of workers as Soviet art and cinema have portrayed it. A few shells were lobbed, some shots were fired, one window was broken, and the leaders of the government were escorted to the prison across the river.

Palace Square

Palace Square (Дворцовая площадь – Dvortsovaya ploshchad) has always been a place for gatherings, both ceremonial and oppositional. Here the tsars greeted troops and celebrated civic and religious holidays, and here on 'Bloody Sunday' (9 January 1905), a group of peaceful workers led by a priest came to the square with a petition for the tsar (not in residence at the time) and were fired on by troops, igniting the first 1905 revolution. Here Leningraders celebrated the end of the war, and here thousands rallied to express their solidarity with Boris Yeltsin in 1991. Today it is where New Year's and other holidays are celebrated, where rock concerts are held – and where teenagers practise their skateboarding techniques.

In the centre of the square is the extraordinary **Alexander Column**, all 600 tonnes rising up 47.5m (156ft) and held aloft by gravity alone. Topped with a bronze angel, the column was designed by Auguste de Montferrand in 1834 in commemoration of the 1812 victory over Napoleon.

The **General Staff Headquarters** was built in 1819–29 by Carlo Rossi for Nicholas I: a magnificent curving building stretching 580m (1,903ft) that seems to embrace and complete the vast open space. It is cut with a gigantic arch topped with Victory in her chariot. The **General Staff Headquarters Museum** (Музей Генерального штаба – Muzey Generalnovo shtaba; Dvortsovaya ploshchad 6; open Tue–

The gigantic arch of the General Staff Headquarters

Sun 10am–6pm; admission fee) is spread over several floors of the building, and accessed along squeaky wooden corridors that provide spectacular views of the square. In addition to the elegant private quarters of Count Nesselrode (prime minister under Alexander I and Nicholas I), the museum has an extensive collection of military uniforms and paraphernalia, an extraordinary collection of applied arts, and French art of the 20th century.

The Winter Palace and Hermitage

The **Winter Palace and Hermitage** (Dvortsovaya nab. 34; open Tue–Sun 10.30–6pm; admission fee; tours and audio-guide in English; times for separate tours of the two treasure galleries held daily are marked on boards in the vestibule; <www.hermitagemuseum.org>) were turned into a museum in 1917. When the German armies invaded the USSR in 1941, about two-thirds of the collection were transported to the Urals; the rest was moved to the lower floors. Despite over 30 bomb attacks and devastating destruction due to water, snow and ice, the palaces survived the war.

Over the decades, the museum collection changed – some works were moved to other Soviet museums or sold, others were expropriated from vast private collections or received as 'trophy art' from Germany and Europe in World War II. This last art is still highly contested, but for now it remains.

Three million items

The total holdings over the museum are over 3 million items. Only 5–10 percent of the Hermitage collection is on display in the halls.

Because the palace buildings are set around courtyards, the museum may seem like a confusing labyrinth. The collection is organised by country and era, and the plan available at the information desk makes navigation easy.

First (ground) floor

The ground floor displays the museum's excellent collections of works from antiquity, including some spectacular Roman statuary and mosaics, as well as fine and applied art from ancient Egypt, the Caucasus and the ancient East. The treasure gallery is divided into two sections. The first displays the breathtaking Scythian gold that dates to the third century BC, as well as gold treasures from later periods. The second section displays work from Byzantium to the 20th century, including imperial jewels and works by Lalique and Fabergé.

Bust of Hermes from the antiquities collection

Second floor

On the second floor of the Winter Palace are state rooms, private quarters, ballrooms and other living areas of the imperial families. The living quarters on the far west side include the rooms that the last Romanov children lived in, a wonderful **Oak Library**, and the **Small Dining Room** where the Provisional Government was arrested by the Bolsheviks. Past the **Dark Corridor** – lined with tapestries and once lit by holes in the floor of the third-floor corridor above it, which was itself illuminated by lanterns on the roof – are the **Golden Drawing Room** and a number of sumptuous boudoirs and sleeping chambers. The state rooms are largely on the Neva side of the palace. In the **Great Hall** (or Nicholas Hall), the largest room in the palace, 5,000 guests could gather and dance. The **Peter the Great Hall** (also called the Small Throne Room) has an English silver-gilt throne made in 1731 and now displays temporary exhibitions.

Perhaps the most spectacular space in the Winter Palace is not a room, but a staircase: the great **Jordan Staircase** built by Rastrelli in 1762. Gracefully proportioned and lavishly decorated in the baroque style, it was originally called the Ambassadorial Staircase, since ambassadors used it to ascend to see the tsar. But it became the Jordan Staircase because it was used by the imperial family to descend to the Neva on Epiphany (celebrated before the revolution on 6 January), the church holiday that celebrates Christ's christening in the Jordan river. On this holiday a hole would be cut in the Neva, from which water would be drawn in a special cup, blessed by the Metropolitan – St Petersburg's religious leader – and drunk by the tsar.

The magnificent Jordan Staircase

The second floors of the buildings display the majority of the museum's vast art collection: French art of the 15th–18th centuries (including works by Poussin, Lorrain and Fragonard); Spanish art (including several canvases by El Greco, the pride of which is *The Apostles Peter and Paul*); the British collection (a particularly large collection of portraits); the German, Dutch and Flemish collections (which include 40 works by Rubens, canvases

Raphael's *Holy Family*

by van Dyck, and an enormous number of paintings by Rembrandt); and the famed collection of Italian art. Here you can find works by Titian, Michelangelo, two canvases by Leonardo da Vinci, including his *Madonna Benois*, and works by Raphael. Other rooms contain extensive collections of medieval European art and armour.

On the second floor of the **Little Hermitage** is the **Pavilion Hall** – an enormous gilded room that overlooks the Hanging Gardens planted under Catherine the Great. The room, lit by nearly 30 chandeliers, has Roman and Byzantine mosaics on the floor and the spectacular **Peacock Clock** made by James Fox in 1772. On the hour the peacock spreads its wings, and a rooster, owl and mushrooms begin to move. When working, it is demonstrated every Wednesday at 5pm.

Third floor

The third floor displays the collection of 19th- and 20th-century art, mostly from private collections expropriated after the

Henri Matisse's *Red Room*

1917 revolution. Here are dozens of works by Monet, Renoir, Degas, Pissarro, Van Gogh, Matisse (including *La Danse*, painted in 1909–10) and Picasso. This floor also has one room of 20th-century Russian art (including Kazimir Malevich's *Black Square*). There is also a collection of numismatics and a fine collection of Byzantine and Eastern fine and applied arts.

East towards the Summer Gardens

The area east of Palace Square is filled with people, shops and arcades, museums, palaces and some of the city's most famous and lovely squares and gardens. This section covers the sight-filled area around the Moika river bounded by the Fontanka in the east and stretching to the Neva river in the north.

Near Palace Square on the Moika river is the **Apartment Museum of Alexander Pushkin** (Музей-квартира А.С. Пушкина – Muzey-kvartira A.S. Pushkina; open Wed–Mon 11am–5pm, closed last Fri of the month; admission fee), where Russia's premier poet lived and then died in 1837, after fighting a duel to defend his wife's honour. The apartment has been reconstructed on the basis of sketches and is filled with Pushkin's possessions.

The street that starts on Palace Square and runs east is called **Millionaire's Street** (Миллионная улица – Millionannaya ulitsa), named for the lavish mansions owned by the aristocracy. Today it is a bit down at heel, but at the east end stands the impressive **Marble Palace** (Мраморный дворец – Mramorny dvorets; Millionnaya ulitsa 5; open Mon 10am–5pm, Wed–Sun 10am–6pm; admission fee), built by Rinaldi in 1768–85 for Catherine the Great's lover Grigory Orlov. A fine example of early classicism, it is ornamented with over 30 kinds and colours of marble, most spectacularly in the **Grand Staircase**, where the soft hues of marble glow under the crystal chandelier. Today it is part of the Russian Museum, exhibiting a private collection of applied and fine arts from the 18th and 19th centuries and an odd assortment of Russian contemporary art, as well as a collection donated by Peter and Irene Ludwig.

To the south of the Marble Palace is the **Field of Mars** (Марсово Поле – Marsovo Pole), used for military parades and festivities starting in 1805. The Soviets appropriated it as a burial ground for the victims of the 1905 revolution; they added a monument to the **Heroes of the Revolution** in 1919, and then an eternal flame in 1957.

On the east side of the narrow Lebyazhnaya Canal are the **Summer Gardens** (Летный сад – Letny sad; open daily May–Oct 10am–

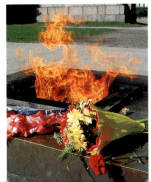

Eternal flame, Field of Mars

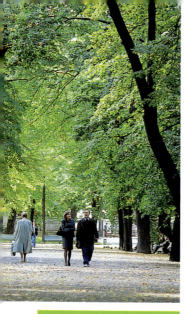

10pm, Nov–Mar 10am–8pm), where Peter the Great built his summer home in a corner of a formal garden with 250 statues and fountains cleverly fed by the river. Although his home survived the disastrous flood of 1777, virtually everything else was destroyed. It was redesigned under Catherine the Great with 92 statues in a natural setting. Throughout the pre-revolutionary period, it was the favourite place for well-born Petersburgers to stroll, chat, flirt and enjoy music and nature. So revered was this garden that not a single tree was felled for firewood during the WWII siege of the city.

In the northeast corner stands Peter's **Summer Palace** (Летный дворец – Letny dvorets; open Mar–Oct Wed–Mon 10am–6pm; admission fee), a marvellous Dutch-style two-storey home built in 1711 by Trezzini. It is filled with carefully preserved artefacts from Peter's life, including a four-poster bed and the cabinets that once held his Cabinet of Curiosities.

The charming neoclassical **Tea and Coffee Houses** are now used to show temporary art and other exhibits.

Pushkin at home

Alexander Pushkin wrote to a friend: 'The Summer Garden is my kitchen garden. I wake up and go there in my robe and slippers. I read, write and take my afternoon nap there. It is home to me.'

Salt Town

To the east of the Fontanka is an area that was once called Salt Town (Соляной городок – Solyanoy gorodok) where the state used to store its supplies of salt and wine. Today it is a lovely neighbourhood of tree-shaded streets notable for two museums. The **Steiglitz Museum**, also called the **Museum of Decorative and Applied Arts** (Музей декоративно-прикладного искусства – Muzey dekorativno-prikladnovo iskusstva; Solyanoy pereulok 13; open Tue–Sat 11am–5pm; admission fee) is part of an industrial design school, founded in 1876 by Baron Alexander Steiglitz. To educate his students, he purchased over 30,000 examples of the finest European and Russian applied arts and commissioned a building from Maximilian Messmacher to display them.

After the 1917 revolution, Steiglitz's collection and school were expropriated, and the palatial halls that imitated rooms in Italian Renaissance, Flemish, baroque and medieval Muscovite style were partitioned or plastered over. The museum is being restored and exhibitions reinstated. Right now it is a jumble of magnificence: glittering halls decorated with tiles, painting and gilding packed willy-nilly with precious European and Russian furniture, ceramics and other applied art from the 16th to 20th centuries.

Next to this museum is the **Museum of the Defence and Blockade of Leningrad** (Музей обороны и блокады Ленинграда – Muzey oborony i blokady Leningrada; Solyanoy pereulok 9; open Tue and Thur–Sun 10am–5pm, closed last Thur of the month; admission fee), opened within months of the lifting of the siege to preserve the memory of those tragic and heroic 900 days. Although there is little in English, most of the extensive exhibitions showing daily life during the blockade and the military operations to take and defend the city are wordlessly eloquent.

NEVSKY PROSPEKT AND AROUND

Nevsky prospekt stretches across the city for 4½km (3 miles) from the Palace Square to the Alexander Nevsky Lavra. It is the city's main artery, filled with people day and night, with shops, cafés, arcades, restaurants and many of the city's main attractions along and off the street. This section describes the sights of Nevsky prospekt from Palace Square in the west to Ploshchad Vostaniya in the east, including a diversion north to Arts Square to take in the excellent Russian Museum and the breathtaking Church 'On Spilled Blood'.

At Palace Square, Nevsky prospekt is a rather dark corridor shadowed by tall buildings. On School No. 210 on the north of the street is a sign preserved from World War II: 'Citizens! This side of the street is more dangerous during a bomb attack!' At the corner of the Politseysky Bridge is the **Literary Café**,

Kazan Cathedral

formerly Wolf and Beranger's, where Pushkin stopped on his way to his fatal duel. On the south corner of Nevksy and the Moika river stands **Stroganov Palace** (Строгановский дворец – Stroganovsky

dvorets; Nevsky 17; open Wed–Sun 10am–6pm, Mon 10am–5pm; admission fee), a baroque masterpiece built by Rastrelli in 1752–4 for the Stroganov family. They lived here until the 1917 revolution. Today nine rooms have been gloriously restored. The rather empty spaces will display temporary exhibitions until the palace becomes a museum of applied arts.

East of the Moika is the pretty **Lutheran Church**, built in the 1830s for the German community (Nevsky 22–24). Made into a vegetable store and then a pool during the Soviet period, it has been returned to the community. On the same (north) side of the street is the landmark *style moderne* former Singer Sewing Machine building (1902–4), now the **House of Books** (Dom Knigi) store.

The glory of this stretch of Nevsky is the **Kazan Cathedral** (Собор Казанской Богоматери – Sobor Kazanskoy Bogomateri; Kazanskaya ploshchad 2; open daily 9am–7.30pm; free), commissioned by Paul I in 1801. Designed by the former serf Andrey Voronikhin to resemble St Peter's in Rome, the classical facade has a sweeping 111m (364ft) curved colonnade that embraces the square before it, which is, incongruously, a traditional political rallying point and teen hang-out. The interior is oddly both spacious and dark, with pink-granite columns and massive chandeliers.

Around Arts Square

The best approach to the lovely **Arts Square** (Площадь Искусств – Ploshchad Iskusstv) is north from Nevsky prospekt along Mikhailovskaya ulitsa, with the elegant Grand Hotel Europe on the western side and the Philharmonic at the corner of Italyanskaya ulitsa to the east. In an oval park stands a 1957 statue of Pushkin; to the west is the Mussorgsky Opera and Ballet Theatre; straight ahead are the classical buildings of the Mikhailovsky Palace. Behind the palace is the **Mikhailovsky Garden**, surrounded by a particularly fanciful wrought-iron fence. The entire square and garden were designed by Rossi in the 1820s.

Mikhailovsky Palace was built in 1819–25 by Rossi for the Grand Duke Michael, and made into a museum of Russian art in 1898. The Benois Wing (named after the architect Leonty Benois) to the west of the main building was constructed in 1914–19 to hold the growing collection (which now numbers over 300,000 pieces of art). Now called the **Russian Museum** (Русский музей – Russky muzey; Inzhenernaya ulitsa 4; open Wed–Mon 10am–5pm; admission fee), it is one of the largest collections of Russian art in the world.

The first floor all three wings (main building, Rossi and Benois) displays art from the earliest icons to the early 20th century. The second floor is largely dedicated to late 19th- and early 20th-century art, as well as folk art and temporary exhibitions.

Statue of Pushkin in Arts Square

The collection of early religious art contains several magnificent icons by Andrey Rublyov (*c.*1340–1430). The academic period (starting in 1757 with the opening of the Academy of Arts) is well represented, with particularly interesting portraits by Dmitry Levitsky and fine seascapes by Ivan Aivazovsky (1817–1900). A rebellion in the Academy in 1863 led to one of Russia's greatest art movements, the Wanderers: a group of artists who travelled around the country paint-

Bust of Peter the Great in the Russian Museum

ing life 'as they saw it' and arranging exhibitions for the masses. Artists like Ilya Repin, Ivan Kramskoy and Nikolay Ge captured Russian life with an almost photographic eye.

In the late 19th century, realism became tempered with lyricism, such as in the landscapes of Isaac Levitan, or romantic historicism, such as in the enormous canvases depicting Russian history by Vasily Surikov or Russian fairy tales and mythology by Viktor Vasnetsov. Mikhail Vryubel and Nikolay Roerich began to pave the way towards the avant-garde with their impressionistic canvases, and the World of Art painters, like Alexander Benois, rebelled against the social conscience of the realist painters with decorative 'art for art's sake'.

At the turn of the 20th century, Russia's social and political upheavals were paralleled by the overturning of great artistic canons by the Russian avant-garde. The museum has a particularly fine collection of avant-garde artworks, in-

The Church of the Resurrection of Christ 'On Spilled Blood'

cluding paintings by Natalya Goncharova, Kazimir Malevich, Vasily Kandinsky and Marc Chagall.

The collection of folk art is very extensive and varied, including toys, embroidery, carvings, ceramics and everyday objects transformed by Russian peasants into fanciful works of art.

Directly to the east of the Russian Museum is the **Museum of Ethnography** (Музей этнографии – Muzey etnografii; Inzhenernaya ulitsa 4/1; open Tue–Sun 10am–5pm, closed last Fri of the month; admission fee), built in 1900–11. Today it has half a million items showing every aspect of daily life over the ages across the territory of the former USSR, with a particularly rich collection of clothing and textiles.

To the northwest of the Russian Museum on the Griboedov Canal is the **Church of the Resurrection of Christ 'On Spilled Blood'** (Храм во имя Воскресения Христова «Спаса на крови» – Khram vo imya Voskreseniya Khristova 'Spasa na krovi'; Konyushnaya ploshchad; open Thur–Tue May–Sept 10.30am–7pm, Oct–Apr 11am–6pm; admission fee). Built on the spot where Tsar Alexander II was mortally wounded in 1881, its bright colours, patterned cupolas, arcades and arches are a bit of medieval Moscow in the northern capital. The interior is entirely covered with mosaics. Only the memorial services for the deceased tsar were held here. During the Soviet period it was a warehouse, but it was reopened in 1997 after nearly 30 years of restoration.

To the east of the Russian Museum is **St Michael's Castle** (Михайловский замок – Mikhailovsky zamok; Sadovaya ulitsa 2; open Mon 10am–5pm, Wed–Sun 10am–6pm; admission fee), built by Paul I with moats and a drawbridge to protect himself from his enemies. It was completed in 1801 (architects Vasily Bazhenov and Vincenzo Brenna), and Paul lived here for exactly 40 days before he was murdered in his bed. In 1825 it was made into the Guards Corps of Engineers School (where the writer Fyodor Dostoevsky studied), and it is often called the **Engineer's Castle**. Now part of the Russian Museum, it has several beautifully restored Pauline rooms (including a glittering throne room and marble-filled church), and displays portraits, works of foreign artists who worked in Russia, and temporary exhibits.

Back on Nevsky Prospekt

Between Griboedov Canal and Sadovaya ulitsa stands the great shopping arcade **Gostiny Dvor** (Nevsky 35; open daily 9am–9pm), built and rebuilt many times over the years to house traders and their wares. The present building was begun by Rastrelli in 1756, completed 1761–85, with the classical porticoes and columns added by Vallin de la Mothe. To the west is the curious **Portik Rusca**, named after architect Luigi Rusca, the entrance to another, less

Gostiny Dvor's shop windows

Lane of symmetry

To see one of the most perfectly proportioned streets in the world, walk behind Ostrovsky Square to Architect Rossi Street (Улица Зодчего Росси – Ulitsa Zodchevo Rossi). The mirror-image arcaded buildings on either side of the street are 22m (72ft) high, exactly 22m (72ft) apart, and the street itself stretches 220m (720ft).

interesting shopping centre. It's located on Dumskaya ulitsa by the striking red **Duma Tower**, built in 1804 as a fire watchtower. Here the city legislature convened before the revolution.

Opposite Gostiny Dvor, set back from the road a little, is the pretty blue-and-white neoclassical **Armenian Church** (Nevsky 40–42), built in 1771–80. Also on the north side of the street are two restored pre-revolutionary arcades, the **Passazh** (Nevsky 48) and **Grand Palace** (Nevsky 44).

Between Sadovaya ulitsa and the Fontanka river on the south side of the road is **Ostrovsky Square** (Площадь Островского – Ploshchad Ostrovskovo), named after Alexander Ostrovsky (1823–86), one of Russia's most prolific and beloved playwrights. Built by Rossi in 1818–39, it is one of the city's centres of the arts. Behind the park and statue of Catherine the Great (erected in 1873) is the magnificent **Alexandrinsky** (also called **Pushkin**) **Theatre**. To the west is the **National Public Library**.

On the east side of Ostrovsky Square is the **Anichkov Palace** (Аничков дворец – Anichkov dvorets), first built by Empress Elizabeth for her lover Razumovsky, and then given by Catherine the Great to her lover Potyomkin. The palace was redesigned many times; the present building owes its rather stolid grey classicism to Rossi. It was later used by the heirs to the throne, although Alexander III liked it so much that he and his family continued to live here. It is now a Children's Cultural Centre.

East of Anichkov Bridge

The **Anichkov Bridge** over the Fontanka river is one of the city's most impressive, adorned at each corner by Pyotr Klodt's sculptures of men taming wild horses. On the southeast side of the Fontanka is the magnificent red baroque **Beloselsky-Belozersky Palace**, built by Andrey Stakenshneider in 1847–8.

On the east side of the Fontanka, some way north of Nevsky prospekt, stands yet another baroque palace of yet another fabulously rich noble family. The **Sheremetev Palace** (Шереметьевский дворец – Sheremetevsky dvorets; Nab. reki Fontanki 34; open Wed–Sun noon–6pm, closed last Wed of the month; admission fee), also called the **Fountain House** (Фонтанный дом – Fontanny dom) for the many fountains that once graced the grounds, was built in 1750–5. The Sheremetevs were great patrons of the arts and supported a serf theatre, so it is fitting that most of the palace is now dedicated to a fantastic collection of musical instruments from every country and virtually every period. The palace rooms are only now being restored, and three chambers are completed.

In the south wing of the palace is the **Anna Akhmatova Museum** (Музей

The pretty Armenian Church is tucked back from the road

Анны Ахматовой – Muzey Anny Akhmatovoy; entrance at Liteyny prospekt 53; open Tue–Sun 10.30am–5.30pm, closed last Wed of the month; admission fee), where this great poet lived from the mid-1920s until 1952. The museum reconstructs several rooms where she and her third husband, Nikolay Punin, lived, and has many manuscripts, personal possessions and portraits.

The stretch of Nevsky prospekt from the Fontanka to **Ploshchad Vostaniya** (Uprising Square) feels a bit more like a generic big-city street, with international chain hotels, restaurants and upscale stores. The square itself, once a poor district that was the starting point for the 1917 revolution, is just a big roundabout by the Moscow Train Station, with a particularly un-Petersburg array of lurid signage, casinos and cafés.

An interesting museum for literature-lovers is the **Dostoevsky Memorial Museum** (Музей-квартира Ф.М. Достоевского – Muzey-kvartira F.M. Dostoevskovo; Kuznechny pereulok 5/2, Apt 119; open Tue–Sun 11am–6pm, closed last Wed of the month; admission fee), south of Nevsky prospekt, where this chronicler of the darker side of St Petersburg's lived the last years of his life in middle-class comfort.

Anna Akhmatova

Anna Akhmatova (1889–1966) was one of the most celebrated poets of the Silver Age. Her first husband, the poet Nikolay Gumilyov, was executed in the first years of Soviet power, her third husband, Punin, was arrested and died in the camps, and her son was imprisoned for many years. Her poems about St Petersburg – the glittering city of her youth and the tragic city of her middle years, when she and her loved ones were hounded by the Soviet authorities – are among the finest poetic expressions of the city. Her celebrated Cubism-inspired portrait by Nathan Altman is in the Russian Museum.

The Senate building on the waterfront

THE ENGLISH QUAY AND SOUTHWEST

The neighbourhoods west and southwest of Palace Square include several magnificent monuments and museums along the Neva river, the city's main cathedral, and one of the oldest sections of the city, Kolomna, where quiet residential streets and romantic canals coexist with lavish palaces and the bustle of Theatre Square.

The Admiralty

To the west of Palace Square is yet another symbol of the city: the imposing **Admiralty**. In 1704 Peter had a shipyard built here, and in 1718 part of the original building was given over to the naval ministries. In 1806–23, Andreyan Zakharov rebuilt the structure in high classicism, with statues and bas-reliefs celebrating the naval fleet, and a 72m (236ft) spire topped with a ship weathervane. Since 1917 it has been a

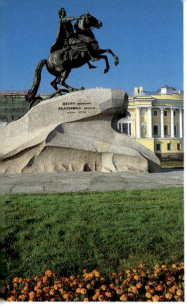

The Bronze Horseman statue in Decembrist Square

naval college and is closed to the public.

However, you can enjoy views of the building from the pretty **Alexandrovsky Park** that stretches from Palace Square to the Manège. Established in 1874 by a botanist, it is filled with rare trees and shrubs, as well as a lovely fountain, busts of writers, and a never-ending crowd of dog-walkers, teenage lovers, strolling mothers and tourists.

The park finishes at **Decembrist Square**, named for the ill-fated group of noblemen *(see page 16)* who staged a rebellion here by the buildings of the **Synod** (of the Russian Orthodox Church) and **Senate** on the west side of the square. These lovely classical buildings, joined with an arch topped by a sculptural group of the goddess of Justice, were built in 1829–36 by Carlo Rossi. After serving as the historical archives during the Soviet period, they are now being refitted as the Constitutional Court, set to move north from Moscow in 2008. Next to the Synod and Senate buildings is the **Manège** (Конногвардейский манеж – Konnogvardeysky manezh; Isaakievskaya ploshchad 1; open Wed–Sun 10am–6pm), built by Giacomo Quarenghi in 1804–7 to stable and train the imperial horse guards. It is now an exhibition centre.

Near the Neva river bank in Decembrist Square is St Petersburg's most famous monument to Peter the Great, usually called the **Bronze Horseman** (Медный всадник – Medny vsadnik). Catherine the Great commissioned Etienne Falconet to design and build it, and after nearly 12 years of artistic quarrelling, it was erected in 1782. While Falconet designed and sculpted the monument, the face of Peter the Great was done by Marie-Anne Collot, Falconet's 18-year-old apprentice. The monument is dedicated 'To Peter I from Catherine II' in Russian and Latin, and depicts Peter the Great trampling the snake of treason under his steed's hoof. The enormous podium of granite the statue rests on is called the Thunder Stone – a stone that had cracked off a cliff when hit by lightning. It weighs over 1,500 tonnes and was hauled here over nine months by 400 men, who moved it about 150m (492ft) a day.

The English Quay and Beyond

The stretch of embankment to the west of Decembrist Square is called the **English Quay** (Английская набережная – Angliyskaya naberezhnaya) since it was the original site of the British embassy. It was one of the city's most prestigious addresses, lined with magnificent palaces and mansions, one of which is now the wonderful **Museum of**

The Bronze Horseman

The statue of Peter the Great is called the Bronze Horseman after a poem by Alexander Pushkin written in 1833. In the poem a young man looses his beloved in a great flood, and in his delirium imagines that the statue leaps off the pedestal and chases him through the city. While praising the city and Peter's vision, the poem suggests that the 'little people' suffer from the whims and ambitions of their leaders. All the same, it is traditional for brides and grooms to be photographed by the monument after their wedding.

St Petersburg's History (Музей истории города Санкт Петербурга – Muzey istorii goroda Sankt Peterburga; Angliyskaya nab. 44; open Thur–Mon 11am–6pm, Tue 11am–5pm; admission fee), also called the **Rumyantsev House**, after the owner and museum's founder, Nikolay Rumyantsev. The house is a magnificent backdrop to fascinating exhibitions on the city's history, with emphasis on the blockade and early Soviet period, including recreations of rooms, bunkers, stores, kitchens and other everyday venues, in addition to photos, documents, posters, videos and other memorabilia.

Near the museum is Ploshchad Truda, where the Grand Duke Nikolay had a rather austere palace built in 1853–61, which was eventually turned into a school for noblewomen. The **Nikolaevsky Palace** was given to the trade unions after the revolution, and remains their headquarters.

Across the square is the timber-storage warehouse called **New Holland** (Новая Голландия – Novaya Gollandiya), founded by Peter the Great in 1719. Rebuilt in 1765, it finally fell out of service and was devastated by fire several years ago.

Golden glory

Over 400kg (882lbs) of gold, 1,000 tonnes of bronze, 16,000kg (32,000lbs) of malachite and eleven sq m (118 sq ft) of lapis, in addition to marble, porphyry and other stones were used in the interior to create columns, statues and mosaics. The 101.5m (333ft) high cathedral can hold 14,000 worshippers.

St Isaac's Square

St Isaac's Square is one of the city's grandest spaces, with the cathedral rising up at one end, the Mariinsky Palace at the other, and a **Monument to Nicholas I** in the centre. The statue was sculpted by Pyotr Klodt in 1859. Images of Faith, Wisdom, Justice and Strength surround the pedestal with scenes from the tsar's reign.

St Isaac's golden dome

It is positioned in front of the **Mariinsky Palace**, built by Nicholas I for his daughter Maria. Since the late 19th century, the palace has housed municipal councils and administrations. The square is lined with pleasantly proportioned buildings, including the famous **Astoria Hotel**, opened in 1910.

The square is dominated by **St Isaac's Cathedral** (Исаакиевский собор – Isaakievsky sobor; Isaakievskaya ploshchad 1; open Thur–Tue 11am–7pm, colonnade open 11am–6pm; admission fee). Named in honour of St Isaac of Dalmatia, whose feast day is celebrated on the day Peter the Great was born, this cathedral was designed and built by Auguste de Montferrand in 1817–58. It is one of the world's largest single-domed churches (the interior dome is 21.8m/70.5ft in diameter), and certainly one of the most lavishly imposing, from its classical exterior with eclectic neo-Renaissance and baroque ornamentation, 112 granite columns holding up the pediments, and huge dome.

The Blue Bridge on the Moika

The church is a rather typical Petersburgian blend of East and West. It is a traditional Russian cross-plan church, but displays religious arts that were more commonly used in the West, such as the extraordinary stained-glass window of the *Resurrected Christ* in the sanctuary, the naturalistic frescos, painted by some of the finest artists of the times, and the bronze and gilded statuary in the lavish interior.

Kolomna

The area to the southwest of St Isaac's Square between the Moika and Fontanka rivers is called Kolomna, named for the workers from the town of Kolomenskoe who settled here. One of the oldest parts of the city, it remained decidedly lower-class until the mid-19th century. It is a pleasant area for strolling, especially along the winding Moika river and Griboedov Canal. The latter has some of the city's most fanciful bridges, like the gilded griffins of the Bank Bridge (so called because of the nearby bank, now an institute), or the lions of the Lion Bridge at Maly Podyacheskaya ulitsa.

The most famous palace on the Moika river is the **Yusupov Palace** (Юсуповский дворец – Yusupovsky dvorets; Nab. reki Moiki 94; open daily 11am–5pm, tours of the cellar in Russian at 1.45pm), the only palace in the city that survives with much of its original interior intact. The fabulously wealthy Nikolay Yusupov purchased an older palace on this site in 1830. Over the years he and his descendants remodelled it to hold their art collection and satisfy their changing tastes. They later added a 'home theatre' that is like the Mariinsky in miniature. By the time the family fled Russia during the 1917 revolution, the palace was an eclectic mélange of styles, from classicism to Renaissance to Rococo to Art Nouveau to Moorish motifs.

After the last Yusupovs escaped to Europe and the palace was expropriated by the state, over 1,000 priceless paintings

The Mysterious Murder of Rasputin

The last of the Yusupovs to live in the Yusupov Palace were the rather decadent Felix and his wife, Irina, the niece of Tsar Nicholas II. They seem to have had a happy marriage, although even by today's standards it was unconventional: in his autobiography, Felix admitted his pleasure in dressing in women's clothing and spending the night carousing. Certainly nothing indicated that Felix was destined to play a key role in Russian history. In 1916 he and several accomplices decided to rid Russia of the greatest threat to the empire: Grigory Rasputin. One December night, the conspirators lured Rasputin to the cellar sitting rooms. They fed him poisoned pastries. When they had no effect, they beat him unconscious. When he ran out of the door, they shot him, and then threw his body in the ice-covered Neva river. Later forensic investigations showed that despite being poisoned, beaten and shot, Rasputin died by drowning.

Statue of Rimsky-Korsukov in Theatre Square

and rare manuscripts were found hidden behind a secret door in Felix's book-lined study. They were eventually distributed to other state museums, but much of the palace remains as it was on the eve of the revolution, with dozens of luxurious and richly decorated public and private rooms open to visitors and often used for concerts and events.

Theatre Square

In the 18th century the imperial family decided to build a new centre for the performing arts on a square that traditionally held fairs and festivals. Theatre Square is home to the **Mariinsky Theatre** and the **Rimsky-Korsukov Conservatory**. The Mariinsky was originally built in 1860, but the present mint-green neo-Renaissance exterior was designed in 1883–96. The interior is a lush, frothy mix of blue, gold and white. The Conservatory, established in 1862 by pianist Anton Rubinshteyn, was completed in 1896.

To the southeast of the square stands the airy blue-and-white **Church of St Nicholas and the Epiphany** (often called Nikolsky Church), one of the city's finest examples of baroque architecture, set between two canals and behind a leafy square. Nearby is another great religious building, the **Choral Synagogue** (Lermontovsky prospekt 2). In 1869 Alexander II approved construction of the temple, although the house of worship was only completed and consecrated in 1893. It was designed in the Moorish style by I. Shaposhnikov, but the heavily ornamented interior was designed by Lev Bachman, the first Jewish graduate of the Academy of Arts.

Nearby is the **Railway Museum** (Музей железнодорожного транспорта – Muzey zheleznodorozhnovo transporta; Sadovaya ulitsa 50; open Sun–Thur 11am–5.30pm, closed last Thur of the month; admission fee), specially constructed in 1901–2 (with additions in 1910–11) to hold a collection of photos, documents, models and even a full-size luxury train from the turn of the 20th century. East of here is **Haymarket Square** (Сенная площадь – Sennaya ploshchad), which used to be the heart of lower-class St Petersburg. It has now been reconstructed into a bustling shopping area that evokes nothing of its notorious past.

Ballet and Ballets Russes

Ever since Jean-Baptiste Landé was invited to Russia in 1738 to train dancers for what would become the famed Imperial Ballet School, 'Russia' and 'ballet' have been synonymous. The Russian school of ballet produced brilliant dancers, such as Anna Pavlova, Vaslav Nijinsky, Rudolf Nureyev and Mikhail Barishnikov, and the brilliant choreographer Maurius Petipa, who choreographed over 60 ballets over his long life (1818–1910).

After the 1917 revolution, many of the Mariinsky and imperial dancers were eager to leave the country, and were snapped up by Sergey Diaghilev for his Ballets Russes. For his innovative ballets Diaghilev combined such choreographers as Michel Fokine and set-designers like Leon Bakst, Alexander Benois, composers like Igor Stravinsky and dancers like Nijinsky. The troupe, which existed from 1909 to 1929, never performed in Russia.

However, the tradition of imperial training continued under the Soviet regime, languishing in the darkest days of Stalinism, but flourishing once again in the 1960s and 1970s in what was now called the Kirov Theatre. Today the troupe continues to dance under the name Kirov, although the theatre is once more called the Mariinsky.

FURTHER AFIELD

The eastern part of the city, north of Nevsky prospekt between Ploshchad Vostaniya and the Alexander Nevsky Lavra, is a quiet part of the city with a few spectacular sights scattered rather far and wide. To the northeast across the Neva is the Vyborg Side, home to the main memorial cemetery that is the final resting place of the victims of the blockade. Southern St Petersburg is a part of the city that visitors usually zip through on their way to and from the airport, but there are several interesting monuments here worth a longer look.

Smolny

The Smolny neighbourhood is to the north of Nevsky prospekt as it runs east from Ploshchad Vostaniya. Named for the tar pits (смола – *smola* in Russian) once here, it is a quiet, predominantly residential neighbourhood. In 1748 the Empress Elizabeth planned to build a spectacular baroque convent, designed by Rastrelli to have a soaring bell tower, cupolas and walls. (The model, which itself took seven years to build, is in the Academy of Arts, *see page 38*.) All she succeeded in building was some of the convent buildings and the breathtaking blue-and-white confection of the **Smolny Cathedral** (Смольный собор – Smolny sobor; Ploshchad Rastrelli 3/1; open Fri–Wed 11am–5pm; admission fee), whose five cupolas rise majestically over the river. Catherine the Great halted the funding and had Ivan Stasov design the interiors in her favourite neoclassical style. Closed as a house of worship after the revolution, the interiors were stripped,

Son of Smolny

The most famous former resident of the Smolny neighbourhood is President Vladimir Putin, who grew up in a communal apartment at Baskov pereulok 12.

View of the Neva from the roof of Smolny Cathedral

and now their disappointingly plain white walls are the back-drop for temporary art exhibitions and concerts.

Nearby is another 'Smolny' – the former **Smolny Institute for Noblewomen**, built by Quarenghi in 1806–8. It was the Bolshevik headquarters right after the revolution, where Vladimir Lenin lived with his wife, Nadezhda Krup-skaya. The building is still used as the centre of city govern-ment and is not open to visitors.

Not far from the cathedral are the cheerful red-and-white **Kikin's Chambers** (Кикины палаты – Kikiny palaty; Stavro-polskaya ulitsa 9), a fine example of Petrine baroque. Built for one of Peter the Great's companions, Alexander Kikin, 1714–20, they were later used to display the Kunstkamera collection until the museum building was finished on Vasilevsky Island. They are now a music school.

A little further east of the Smolny Cathedral and Institute is the neoclassical **Tauride Palace** (Таврический дворец –

Tavrichesky dvorets; Shpalernaya ulitsa 47), built in 1783–9 by Ivan Starov for Catherine the Great as another palace gift for her favourite, Grigory Potyomkin, after his military success in Crimea (once called Tavria). Today the building hosts the Parliamentary Assembly of the CIS (Commonwealth of Independent States) and is not open to the public, but the lovely natural gardens and lake are open for strolling.

The Alexander Nevsky Lavra

Nevsky prospekt ends in the west at the **Holy Trinity Alexander Nevsky Lavra** (Свято Тройцкая Алексанро-Невская Лавра – Svyato Troytskaya Aleksandro-Nevskaya Lavra; open daily winter 9.30am–5pm, summer 9.30am–7pm; admission fee), founded in 1710 by Peter the Great in honour of Alexander Nevsky. Reached through a gate and path that is lined with the poor and infirm begging for alms, this ac-

Mass at the Holy Trinity Cathedral

tive monastery seems to exist in a different time and place. The oldest church in the monastery is the red-and-white **Church of the Annunciation**, built by Trezzini in 1717–22. The main church, the **Holy Trinity Cathedral**, was built in the neoclassical style by Ivan Starov in 1776–90, with magnificent golden

Royal Gates leading to the sanctuary. A silver-and-gold reliquary with the remains of Alexander Nevsky is to the right of the altar. In 1993 they were returned to the church from the Museum of Religion and Atheism, where they had been kept after the revolution. The monastery was closed from 1922 to 1956, when only one church was allowed to open for services. The monastery was revived in 1994.

Adjoining the monastery are cemeteries where St Petersburg's most important citizens have been buried. In 1932, after the monastery was closed, the state renamed the cemeteries the **Museum of Urban Sculpture** (open Tue–Wed and Fri–Sun 11am–5pm; admission fee) and moved many artistically valuable gravestones here. Among the people interred in these leafy and pleasant grounds are Mikhail Lomonosov, Carlo Rossi, Giacomo Quarenghi, Fyodor Dostoevsky, Mikhail Glinka, Marius Petipa and Pyotr Tchaikovsky.

Anyone who loves the decorative arts should trek south along the Neva to the **Imperial Porcelain Factory Museum** (Музей императорского фарфорового завода – Muzey imperatorskovo farforovovo zavoda; Prospekt Obukhovskoy oborony 151; open Tue–Sat 10.30am–6pm, Sun 10.30am–5pm; admission fee; Lomonosovskaya metro), called the Lomonosov Factory during the Soviet years. Opened in 1744, the factory produced porcelain for the imperial family, and its museum halls display 250 years of porcelain masterpieces. The most breathtaking piece is a large 'Biscuit Bouquet' (unglazed fired porcelain) made in 1850. Every petal is so delicate and lifelike, it's hard to believe it was crafted in clay by human hands.

Vyborg Side

The area north of the eastern part of St Petersburg on the other side of the Neva, called the Vyborg Side, has a few pockets of pretty residential areas amidst a great deal of industrial urban landscape. It is famous for the **Finland Station** (Ploshchad Lenina 6), where Lenin arrived after 17 years plotting revolution in European exile and made his renowned speech on top of an armoured train. The station itself is a grim Soviet replacement, but there is a legendary statue of Lenin in the middle of the square, now surrounded by all the

Statue of Lenin outside Finland Station

detritus of the new capitalist Russia the leader of the proletariat would have despised.

The main reason to visit the Vyborg Side is the cemetery of mass graves where the victims of the blockade were buried. **Piskaryovskoe Cemetery** (Пискарёвское мемориальное кладбище – Piskaryovskoe memorialnoe kladbishche; Prospekt Neprokoryonnikh 72; open daily 10am–5pm; free; metro Lesnaya or Ploshchad Muzhestva) was the place where over

Piskaryovskoe memorial

500,000 bodies were buried in mass graves from 1941–3. In 1960 the memorial complex was redesigned with two memorial halls and the grand mourning figure of Mother Russia by Vera Isaeva and Robert Taurit. On the wall behind it is a poem by Olga Berggolts, which ends with the oft-quoted phrase: 'No one and nothing is forgotten.' Music is broadcast throughout the cemetery, making every visit to this place a pilgrimage.

Southern Suburbs

Joseph Stalin, allegedly revolted by the imperial and aristocratic city centre of St Petersburg, hatched a grandiose plan to move the centre south to Moskovsky prospekt. He managed to initiate work on the enormous 'Stalinist classical' **House of Soviets** (Moskovsky prospekt 2/2), which was completed after the war, but thankfully his grand plan was never brought to completion.

There are three monuments here of considerable historical interest. The enormous 12-columned **Moscow Triumphal**

Arch at Ploshchad Moskovskie Vorota was built by Vasily Stasov in 1838 to commemorate the Russo-Turkish War. Another triumphal arch further west, the **Narva Triumphal Gate** (Ploshchad Stachek) was designed by Quarenghi and erected in 1814 to commemorate victory over Napoleon's armies. It was redesigned and built by Vasily Stasov in 1827–34, with a magnificent sculptural group of the goddess of Victory in her chariot led by six horses, sculpted by Pyotr Klodt, on top.

A monument at Ploshchad Pobedy commemorates the **Defenders of Leningrad**. This huge sculptural group includes 34 bronze figures. Under the monument is a museum about the blockade (Монумент героическим защитникам Ленинграда – Monument geroicheckim zashchitnikam Leningrada; open Tue–Sun 10am–5pm, closed last Tue of the month, by appointment; tel: 812-293 6563; free), which has 900 bronze sheets chronicling the siege, lit by 900 bronze lamps, as a metronome beats out the city's heartbeat, just as it did on the radio during the blockade.

The southern part of the city also has one extraordinary religious monument – the **Chesma Church** (Чесменская церковь – Chesmenskaya tserkov; Ulitsa Lensoveta 12; open daily 10am–7pm; free) built 1777–80 by Yuti Felten and named in honour of the Battle of Çesme in the Russo-Turkish War. The only neo-Gothic church in the city, its red facade with thin vertical lines of white moulding, tower-like cupolas and unusual shape are an aesthetic shock in this otherwise undistinguished neighbourhood.

Unusual Chesma Church

The Grand Palace at Peterhof

PALACE EXCURSIONS

The 'necklace' of palaces that ring the city are even more magnificent than the imperial domiciles in the city centre. Almost all of them were occupied and destroyed by the German armies in World War II, although most of the furnishings, art and fittings were evacuated in advance. What you see today is a double miracle: the breathtaking beauty of the original buildings and parks, and the astonishing work of thousands of restorers who have been bringing this beauty back to life from the ashes and rubble.

Peterhof

In 1709 Peter the Great began to build a palace overlooking the Gulf of Finland. He then changed his vision after visiting Versailles in 1717. **Peterhof** (Петергоф; open daily 11am–5pm; Grand Palace closed Mon and last Tue of the month;

Samson opening the jaws of the lion, part of the Great Cascade

other buildings closed on various days; all buildings open Fri–Sun; fountains open May–Sept; admission fee) was built and rebuilt many times, most notably under the luxury-loving Elizabeth and her court architect Rastrelli. Parts of the **Grand Palace** (first built in 1714–25 by the architects Braunstein, Zemtsov and Le Blond, and then rebuilt and expanded by Rastrelli in 1745–55) are still under restoration, but the dozens of restored rooms, with their original art, furnishing and chandeliers in place, are breathtaking. Also in the grounds is the charming **Monplaisir** (1714–22), the small 'cottage' where Peter the Great preferred to stay, the **Marly Palace**, the neo-Gothic **Cottage Palace** (1826–9) and the **Hermitage** (1721–5) – a pink-and-white confection surrounded by a moat. This was a private dining room with a table that could be raised and lowered from the kitchen below, fully set and covered with food and drink.

These palaces are set on nearly 600 hectares (1,500 acres) of formal and landscaped parks, filled with fountains. The masterpiece is the **Great Cascade**: 64 fountains, 142 water jets and 37 gold statues, including the magnificent **Statue of Samson** opening the jaws of the lion (an allegory for Peter's victory over the Swedes). There are 144 fountains in the park, ranging from the magnificent to the silly – like hidden fountains set off by footsteps. They are fed by 40km (25 miles) of pipes without a single pump – a unique feat of aquatic engineering.

Tsarskoe Selo

In the 18th century, about 25km (16 miles) to the south of St Petersburg, there was a Finnish estate called Saari-mois, or Sarskaya myza in Russian, which meant 'farmstead on a promontory'. After going through several hands, the property was given to Catherine I, the wife of Peter the Great, who had a stone cottage and formal gardens built. When her daughter the Empress Elizabeth inherited it, she commissioned Rastrelli to build an enormous summer palace there, named the **Catherine Palace** (open daily 10am–5pm; palace open Wed–Mon 10am–4.30pm, closed last Wed of the month; Cameron Gallery open Wed–Mon 10am–5pm, closed last Mon of the month; admission fee) in honour of her mother. She spent 1.2 million roubles on the palace and parks, including over 100kg (220lbs) of gold on the interior and exterior ornamentation. The second Catherine ('the Great') had Charles Cameron build neo-classical additions to the original baroque structure. Over the centuries, the village name Sarskaya myza changed to Tsarskoe selo (the tsar's village).

Today, much of Rastrelli's robin-egg-blue-and-gold palace has been restored, including the spectacular

The golden domes of the Catherine Palace

In the Amber Room

Great Hall, lined with mirrors and windows covered with carved, gilded wood, and the 'eighth wonder of the world', the recreated **Amber Room**.

The expansive grounds of the palace (nearly 560 hectares/ 1,400 acres) include the original formal gardens and the natural **Landscaped Gardens** commissioned by Catherine the Great, with beautiful buildings, pavilions and sculptures nestled into the gentle hills and around the **Great Pond**. One of the most beautiful neoclassical structures in Russia is the **Cameron Gallery**, designed by Charles Cameron in 1783–7. Here Catherine held formal dinners by the rows of busts of Greek and Roman heroes (and one Russian – the scientist and philosopher Mikhail Lomonosov).

Attached to the Catherine Palace by an arch is the **Lycée** (Sadovaya ulitsa 2; open Wed–Mon 10.30am–4.30pm, closed last Fri of the month), founded in 1811 to provide classical education to the upper classes. The Lycée has been restored and is a museum showing the classrooms, rather Spartan dormitory rooms and imposing public halls of Russia's foremost academy. Russia's premier poet, Alexander Pushkin, studied here and then lived in the town with his wife in a small wooden cottage that is now the charming **Pushkin Dacha Museum** (Мемориальный музей-дача А.С.Пушкина – Memorialny muzey-dacha A.S. Pushkina; Pushkinskaya ulitsa 2/19; open Wed–Sun 10.30am–5.30pm, closed last Fri of the month; admission fee). During the Soviet period, the town was renamed Pushkin in honour of the poet.

The Amber Room

The original Amber Room was made in 1701–9 for the Charlottenburg Palace of Friedrich I of Prussia. In 1716, Peter the Great admired it and, as legend has it, bought it in exchange for 55 grenadier soldiers and his personal drinking mug. The room was shipped to St Petersburg and first installed in the Winter Palace, but Empress Elizabeth had it moved to the Catherine Palace and invited German and Russian artisans to enlarge the panels to fit the more spacious room. Over 6 tonnes of intricately carved, brilliantly coloured amber covered 55 sq m (592 sq ft).

Because the fragile and brittle amber could not be moved easily, before World War II Russian curators covered the walls with wallpaper to hide the treasure from the German army. This ruse did not work, and when the palace came under attack, the Germans disassembled it in 36 hours and shipped it out. That was the last anyone saw of it, despite hundreds of attempts to find it. The only original piece found was one of the Florentine mosaic inlays that surfaced in 1997.

In 1979 Russian artisans began to rebuild the magnificent room using old photographs and drawings as their guide. It was dedicated and opened in 2003 during the celebration of St Petersburg's 300th anniversary.

The sumptuous state
bedroom at Pavlovsk

Pavlovsk

Catherine the Great gave her son Paul the lovely land at **Pavlovsk** (Павловск; Ulitsa Revolyutsii 20; open Sat–Thur 10am–5pm, closed first Mon of the month; admission fee) by the Slavyanka river in 1777 to commemorate the birth of her grandson and future tsar, Alexander I. The **Palace**, many of the pavilions and the landscaped English-style park were largely designed by Charles Cameron. The palace is a masterpiece of neoclassicism, with a 64-columned dome dominating its graceful facade. Today it is filled with much of the original furniture and art (including some from Gatchina, another Pauline palace), making it one of the most interesting residences for lovers of the applied arts.

The **Park** in which the palace is set is particularly beautiful, with rolling hills, ponds and the winding river Slavyanka. Originally it was filled with galleries for songbirds and gardens of roses, Paul's wife Mariya's favourite flower. Of particular interest are the **Apollo Colonnade**, designed by Cameron in 1782–3 as an artfully created ruin, and the **Temple to Friendship**, which was commissioned by Mariya in 1780 to ensure warm relations with her mother-in-law, the Empress Catherine. Today Pavlovsk continues to celebrate Mariya's love of roses with an annual rose festival in June.

Strelnya: The Constantine Palace

Strelnya: The Constantine Palace (open Tue–Sun 10am–5pm by appointment or tour only, *see page 117*, closed last Tue of the month). Strelnya was the first site Peter the Great contemplated for his Russian Versailles. In 1721 he began to build a **Palace**, and then abandoned it when he decided on the site at Peterhof. It had many owners before the revolution, including the Grand Dukes Constantine (younger sons of Paul and Nicholas I). After the revolution, it was used by many organisations, destroyed by the German armies, partially rebuilt and then abandoned after a fire in 1986. In 2001 the Russian government decided it was just what was needed for the Group of Eight summit, and in a mere 18 months the entire palace and grounds were reconstructed, complete with helicopter pad and a hotel of 20 cottages for the visiting dignitaries.

Today it is not a museum, but an official governmental residence (which means a security detail troops along with the tourists). The fun of it is seeing the spectacularly reconstructed palace rooms, both grand and intimate, where the presidents of the eight great world powers and other leaders held their formal and informal meetings. Of particular interest is the **Belvedere Room**, designed like a cosy ship's cabin at the top of the palace, where Mr Bush and Mr Putin chatted, and the Dutch-style **Kitchen** down below, where Mr Putin entertained such leaders as Italian Premier Berlusconi and German Chancellor Shröder.

Milestones

On the roads leading out of St Petersburg are stone markers called вёрсты – *vyorsty*, marking each *vyorst* (1.6km or about 1 mile) from the capital.

WHAT TO DO

St Petersburg by night is as captivating as St Petersburg by day. For lovers of the classical performing arts, the city offers so much dance, music and theatre in such breathtaking venues that it will be hard to decide where to go. For visitors with more contemporary musical tastes, there are a plethora of clubs, bars and concert halls with everything from reggae to techno. You can take a respite from museums by shopping for bargains (still to be had) in pre-revolutionary arcades or street stalls, or stroll through some of the city's parks, take in a football game, or indulge in the Venice of the North's best way to sightsee: a boat tour that cruises the canals. And if you come with children, you'll find the city to be child-friendly and filled with all kinds of activities for the kids.

ENTERTAINMENT AND NIGHTLIFE

Performances and concerts usually begin at 7pm, precluding a pre-theatre dinner, but there are stands in virtually all the theatres and concert halls that open before the performance and during intermissions selling sandwiches, drinks and pastries. Coats and large bags must be checked in. Tickets can be purchased at the box offices at the theatres, at theatre kiosks around the city or through hotel service desks. Note that tickets for the Mariinsky are only sold at the well-marked outlet on the second floor of Gostiny Dvor (the southeast corner where all the tour buses gather). Touts usually have tickets furtively for sale at the prime venues.

Inside the Mariinsky Theatre

Opera, Dance and Music

The classical performing arts, nurtured, supported and sponsored by the imperial families for centuries, continue to maintain the highest levels of artistry and professionalism. The Mariinsky Theatre (Teatralnaya ploshchad 1; tel: 812-326 4141) is home to the famous Kirov Ballet (the troupe kept the more familiar Soviet name), under the artistic direction of Valery Gergiev. Across the street, the Conservatory (Teatralnaya ploshchad 3; tel: 812-571 0506) holds some of the best concerts in the city. The Mussorgsky Opera and Ballet (Ploshchad Iskusstv 1; tel: 812-595 4284) and Philharmonic (Mikhailovskaya ulitsa 2; tel: 812-710 4257) also have high-quality performances. The lovely Academic Capella (Nab. reki Moiki 20; tel: 812-314 1058) holds concerts and festivals.

Some of the most divine musical evenings are to be had in former palaces and cathedrals. The airy Smolny Cathedral is a concert hall (Ploshchad Rastrelli 3/1; tel: 812-577 1421) that holds many concerts of religious music. And the concerts in the Hermitage Theatre, Yusupov and Anichkov palaces are as much a celebration of the famous halls as the music itself.

Theatre

St Petersburg was the thetrical centre of the empire until Stanislavsky and Nemerovich-Danchenko changed the world

Queue tip

In the large theatres and halls you can rent opera glasses from the cloakroom attendant; even if you don't need them, take them: people returning binoculars get to jump to the head of the queue to get their coats.

of drama with their Moscow Art Theatre, after which the theatrical lights seemed to burn a bit more brightly in the southern capital. But theatregoing is still a joy in St Petersburg, even if you can't understand much: the halls themselves, as well as the rituals of champagne and smoked salmon during the intermissions, make the entire experience a theatrical event. For classic theatre, try the Pushkin Theatre (more commonly known as the Alexandrinsky) or the Bolshoy Dramatic Theatre. More innovative drama can be found at Lev Dodin's Maly Dramatic Theatre.

Nightlife

Russians are jazz fiends. Ever since the first jazz band appeared in 1922, they have been tapping their feet to excellent jazz, both home-grown and imported. The classic jazz site in St Petersburg is the Jazz Philharmonic

Russian ballet

(Zagorodny prospekt 27), or the Jazz Time Bar (Mokhovaya ulitsa 41). For good Armenian food and mellow music, try the Neo Jazz Club (Solyanoy pereulok 14). Oddly, reggae, like sushi, has been adopted by Russians and has a big following. For a fun evening of reggae, check out Jambala (Bolshoy prospekt 80). For old-time rock and roll fans, St Petersburg was once the hub of the underground rock scene, and no performance by the groups DDT or Aquarium should be missed.

The club scene changes frequently, so be sure to check local listings for the *au courant* hang-out. Perennial favourites are the American-run City Bar (Furshtatskaya 20), Griboedov Bunker (Voronezhsakaya ulitsa 2A) or Manhattan (Nab. reki Fontanki 90). If you feel like a real party, drop by one of the

Anyone for vodka?

two Purga bars (Nab. reki Fontanki 11); the waiting staff tend to dress up as animals, and every night at midnight everyone celebrates New Year. Casinos often have top pop music acts at the weekend in addition to the usual risky forms of entertainment. Most clubs have an entry fee and some have face control; casinos usually require a minimum purchase of chips to enter.

SHOPPING

St Petersburg still doesn't have truly great boutique shopping, but there are plenty of arcades and shops where you can find good bargains, interesting wares and plenty of souvenirs. Just be sure to buy only contemporary crafts and mementoes: any antiques must be first cleared by the Ministry of Culture before export, and Soviet military medals cannot be taken out of the country at all.

What to Buy

Amber and semi-precious stones. Amber from the Baltic Sea comes in many colours: transparent yellow, creamy gold, dark amber, or even white or green. Semi-precious stones from the Urals and Siberia are also priced well and lovely, especially malachite, lapis lazuli and charoite (a purple stone discovered in the late 20th century by the river Chara).

Ceramics, porcelain and crystal. Some of the finest bone china in the world is still made at the Imperial Factory and can be purchased at excellent prices. Russian crystal is also high-quality and a good bargain. Blue-and-white ceramics from Gzhel are another traditional craft.

Food and drink. Try some flavoured varieties of vodka or a jar of good caviar (best purchased in one of the shops in Gostiny Dvor, and never on the street). Russian chocolates are richer than Western varieties; look for Korkunov or candies from the local Krupskaya chocolate factory.

Fur. St Petersburg is filled with fur stores selling locally designed coats, jackets and hats made from Russian pelts, as well as cheaper goods from Italy, Turkey or Greece. The best hats are fox, mink, sable and karakul, and the best time to buy is in the summer, when prices are low. Check the seams to be sure they are tight, and scrunch the hat to be sure the fur pops up nicely (if it doesn't, the fur may be dried out or old).

Lacquer boxes. Although lacquer boxes seem to be an age-old craft, they were actually begun in the Soviet period when icon-painters transferred their techniques to making these small boxes. The towns of Palekh, Mstera, Fedoskino and Kholuy each have their own styles. To be sure you are buying the real thing, run your finger over the edges of the painting. If it isn't smooth, the image may be an appliqué.

Linen and woollens. St Petersburg has a number of shops selling fine linen – both bed and table linen and

Honeyed promises

If you think honey is sweet, clear, syrupy stuff, think again. Or better yet, step into a store or market selling Russian honey. You'll see dozens of varieties, from transparent acacia honey to opaque brown buckwheat honey, which is slightly bitter. Each kind has its own flavour and special properties, from helping you fall asleep to cleaning out your insides.

clothing. You can also find good lace and embroidery. Paisley scarves come in a plethora of colours and designs, but be sure to ask if they are Russian-made. If you come from a cold climate, look for hand-knitted angora socks, sweaters and scarves.

Soviet memorabilia. There is plenty of Soviet kitsch for sale, from army surplus wares to old banners. Be sure not to buy any military medals or badges, which cannot be exported. Modern watches, flasks and camouflage gear are popular souvenirs.

Toys and dolls. The matryoshka (nesting) doll is said to have been invented in a small town outside Moscow, but it has spread across the country as its most identifiable souvenir. Cost is determined by the number of dolls and the quality of the painting. Another good bargain is carved wooden toys and Christmas tree decorations.

Where to Shop

Artisan and souvenir markets. The main outdoor crafts market in the city is by the Church 'On Spilled Blood', where hundreds of vendors operate from dawn to dusk (and nearly all night during the White Nights). Artists sell their canvases in front of St Catherine's Church (Nevsky prospekt 32–34), and another group does caricatures on Ploshchad Ostrovskovo.

Matryoshka dolls

Pre-revolutionary department stores. The city's shopping Mecca remains Gostiny Dvor (Nevsky prospekt 35), where there are hundreds of little stores selling everything from honey to fur coats to toasters to shampoo. The

A traditional delicatessen on Nevsky prospekt

glass-roofed Passazh (Nevsky prospekt 48) and snazzy Grand Palace (Nevsky prospekt 44) are now classy shopping arcades, with some traditional Russian wares amidst foreign brands.

Gift and souvenir shops. The city boasts many souvenir shops, all of which tend to have the same selection of crafts. The most interesting are Heritage (Nab. reki Moika 37), Onegin (Ploshchad Iskusstv 11), which also sells art, and Nevsky Souvenir (throughout the city). The Amber Cave (Ulitsa Malaya Morskaya 19) has an enormous and varied selection of amber in all colours. The Gallery of Glass (Ulitsa Lomonosova 1/28) offers hand-blown crystal and an interesting assortment of handmade glass, ceramic and enamel art. For good prices on imperial porcelain, the factory store (Prospekt Obukhovskoy oborony 151) can't be beaten. The store has an enormous selection of china (which they can ship for you), including the famous Cobalt Net service (designed in 1950 and based on an imperial pattern). If you have deep pockets, you can order an entire imperial service or have their artists design your own family china. Galereya Kukol (Ulitsa Bolshaya Morskaya 53/8) sells handmade puppets and dolls as well as exhibiting museum-quality pieces. Military paraphernalia can be found at the packed shop on Ulitsa Sadovaya 26.

Books and electronic goods. Dom Knigi (Nevsky prospekt 28) has large selections of art books and posters. The Anglia and John Parsons bookshops (both at Nab. reki Fontanki 38) have large selections of books in English on Russia, as well as paperbacks, maps and guidebooks. The funky art shop at Pushkinskaya 10 (entrance from Ligovsky prospekt 53) has a great collection of art books, posters and cards, with an emphasis on non-conformist art and Soviet kitsch. Dom Knigi and many shops in Gostiny Dvor also have a large selection of films on DVD, as well as computer games and music. Discs sold on the street, in kiosks and at the electronics markets are generally pirated. The music store Open World of Music (Ulitsa Malaya Morskaya 13) offers the best selection of classical music in the city.

Art galleries. St Petersburg's art world has not reassumed the glory of the pre-revolutionary years or risen to the hype of Moscow's, but the lively underground art world of the Soviet years has morphed into an original, inter-

Fur hats

esting and lively art scene. For pretty hard-core, non-conformist art, visit Ulitsa Pushkinskaya 10 (entrance at Ligovsky Prospekt 53). The buildings were originally taken over by squatters in the late 1980s and are now filled with floor after floor of apartments, galleries, studios

and places where artistic happenings are still happening. It is also filled with witty graffiti and extravagantly dressed and coifed young people. For something a bit more down-to-earth, the friendly and savvy SPAS Gallery (Nab. reki Moiki 93) is a small gallery that has been representing a variety of artists for the last ten years. Another friendly salon with a very wide variety of art (from the 1920s) is Sol Art, located in the Steiglitz Museum (Solyanoy pereulok 15). The Marina Gisich Gallery (Nab. reki Fontanki 121/13), Borey Art Gallery (Liteyny prospekt 58) and D-137 Gallery (Nevsky prospekt 90/92) are considered the city's cutting-edge art dealers. All dealers arrange export permissions (and shipping); works purchased on the street for under US$100 are usually not questioned at customs (although customs officials exersise considerable discretion), so ask for a receipt, even handwritten, for any art you purchase.

OUTDOOR ACTIVITIES

Boat Trips

St Petersburg should be seen at least once from the water. During the warm weather there are canal tours with booking offices and boarding points by Nevsky prospekt on the Moika, Griboedov Canal and Fontanka. Larger boats on the

A boat trip cruises under Engineer's Bridge

Neva (booking office and boarding by the Winter Palace) offer tours and a great and comfortable route to Peterhof palace. Water taxis can also be found by Nevsky prospekt; they can either take you quickly from point A to point B, or be hired for a private tour of the canals and rivers.

The most beautiful bridges over the Griboedov Canal are south of Nevsky prospekt: the black-and-gold griffins on the Bank Bridge by ulitsa Lomonsova and the white stone lions on the Lion Bridge by Lviny pereulok, not far from the Mariinsky Theatre. On the Fontanka river, one of the most intricate bridges is the Bridge of St Panteleimon, by the Summer Garden. Its gold-and-black lanterns are topped with double-headed eagles, and it was named for the red early-baroque Church of St Panteleimon (dating to 1722, one of the oldest extant churches in the city) on nearby Ulitsa Pestelya. At the far southern end of the river, where it is crossed by Lomonsovsky prospekt, is the magnificent

Egyptian Bridge, with its black-and-gold sphinxes. It was built in the early 19th century at the height of the city's fascination with ancient Egypt.

Football and Bath Houses

Everybody in St Petersburg loves the Zenit football team, even the police, since the crime statistics go down every time there is an important match. To see what it's all about, you can get a ticket at the Petrovsky stadium box office, through kiosks or from your hotel. If you are a hockey fan, the local team, SKA, plays September–June at the Yubileyny Sports Palace.

Alternatively you can try that quintessential Russian relaxation technique: a visit to a bath house (баня – *banya*). You can rent an entire facility for an evening (ask at your hotel), or visit the Yamskie bath house (Ulitsa Dostoevskovo 9; tel: 812-312 5836; <www.yamskie.ru>), which offers a full range of pampering delights in old-world elegance.

The Venice of the North

The three main waterways on the palace side of the Neva river – the Moika river, Griboedov Canal and Fontanka river – are all crossed by magnificent bridges: some wide enough for traffic and pedestrians, some so narrow they can only be crossed in single file, and all decorated with magnificent wrought-iron railings, statuary and ornamentation.

If you cruise the Moika (or walk along its banks) from the Hermitage to the south, the first one you'll see is the Singer's Bridge with its intricately formed railings. This was once painted bright yellow, and further south were other bridges painted red and blue. Near the Yusupov Palace is the Lantern Bridge with lamp-posts styled as treble clefs. Further south, near the Kryukov Canal and the ghostly New Holland is the Kisses Bridge, named for a tavern that once stood nearby, which presumably offered more than pub grub to its patrons.

CHILDREN'S ST PETERSBURG

St Petersburg is great for kids – there are plenty of ships and cannons to clamber on – not to mention creepy squiggly things in the Kunstkamera and trick fountains at Peterhof.

Bolshoy Puppet Theatre (Ulitsa Nekrasova 10; tel: 812-273 6672). Established in 1931, this great theatre has nearly 20 different shows.

Demmeni Marionette Theatre (Nevsky prospekt 52; tel: 812-571 2156). This puppet theatre is the oldest in Russia, founded in 1918. It later merged with another puppet theatre directed by the brilliant puppet master Yevgeny Demmini. The theatre's repertory consists of 15 pieces in various styles and genres, based on the works of both Russian and foreign authors.

St Petersburg State Circus (Nab. reki Fontanki 3; tel: 812-570 5390). The St Petersburg Circus – and with it many of the renowned Russian circus arts – was founded in 1877 in the first stone circus building in Russia. The founder was an Italian circus performer and trainer, Gaetano Ciniselli. Over the decades the acts have become more spectacular.

Puppet Fairy-Tale Theatre (Moskovsky prospekt 12; tel: 812-388 0031). Another top theatre with puppets and actors in flamboyant costumes.

Leningradsky Zoo (Alexandrovsky park 1; tel: 812-232 8260). Old Russian zoos are only slowly being redesigned for maximum animal comfort. This zoo was opened in 1865 and is home to nearly 2,000 creatures.

Fun in the snow

Calendar of Events

Christmas and New Year Christmas Musical Encounters in Northern Palmyra classical musical festival (held at the two halls of the Philharmonic) and the Arts Square Musical Festival, which is also held at the Philharmonic.

February The Mariinsky's annual ballet festival. The week before Lent is Maslenitsa (Butter Week), a wild celebration of bliny-eating and festivities, celebrated around the city and in suburban parks.

April The Sergey Kuryokhin International Festival (<www.kuryokhin.ru>), named after and in honour of a talented avant-garde composer and musician who died in 1996.

May The Peterhof fountains are opened with a bang on the first weekend. City Day (last weekend) with city-wide festivities, outdoor concerts, and special events at the Peter and Paul Fortress.

June–August White Nights festival with a plethora of musical and cultural events for all tastes. In June you can attend the Klezfest of East European Jewish folk music, the Stars of the White Nights Classical Music Festival (which is held from late May through August), the White Nights Swing Jazz Festival, not to mention the White Nights Rock Music Festival. Film-lovers might enjoy the Message to Man Festival of short, animated and documentary films (<www.message-to-man.spb.ru>) and the Festival of Festivals (<www.filmfest.ru>), an international film festival, both held in June. In Tsarskoe selo there is an annual carnival on the last weekend in June.

July Navy Day (first Sunday after 22 July) fills the Neva with ships, boats and submarines, as does August Sailing Week.

September The Peterhof fountains celebrate a spectacular dance, music, light and fireworks extravaganza (second weekend). The new performing arts season begins in September, usually with a number of high-profile premieres. The Early Music Festival (<www.earlymusic.ru>) performs rare works in late September to early October.

November The Sound Ways Modern Music Festival brings more avant-garde music to the city.

EATING OUT

When Peter the Great moved his court up north to St Petersburg, his noblemen brought with them their customs, culture and cuisine. Although the city is much further north, the displaced Muscovites had at their disposal the same root vegetables, game and fish, and used their recipes from home. Over the centuries this traditional peasant-hearty Russian cuisine was modified by European cuisines, particularly French, which was reflected in richer and more complex dishes – notably buttery and creamy pastries.

Despite the stagnation of the Soviet era, St Petersburg still has a fine tradition of pre-revolutionary restaurants and an elegant European-inspired cuisine. Today you can find cuisine from virtually every country and nation on earth, but the best restaurants are celebrating their native cuisine with traditional and updated recipes in settings that have been restored to their previous grandeur.

Where to Eat

Although there are a variety of good restaurants all over the city, many are concentrated near the major squares, and particularly along and around Nevsky prospekt. Restaurants specifically catering to foreign tourists are usually below-par, but virtually every café or restaurant has an English menu.

Look for signs for the бизнес-ланч (business lunch); these prix-fixe meals of starter, soup, main and a drink are an excellent bargain. For a quick and cheap bite to eat, the city's many bliny shops can't be beaten. Or stop in a bar café for some good local beer (пиво – *pivo*) and a traditional order of boiled crayfish (раки – *raki*) or shrimp (креветки – *krevetki*), or the guilty pleasure of garlic toast (сухарики – *sukhariki*) – bread buttered, coated with garlic and fried until crunchy.

When to Eat

Breakfast is usually served from about 7am to noon. The lunch hour stretches from noon to 4pm, and dinner is usually served from 6 to 11pm (sometimes until the last customer), although most restaurants only get crowded after 7 or 8pm. All day long you can stop in a coffee shop (кофейня – *kofeynya*) for coffee, tea and sweet and savoury treats, or a bliny shop for pancakes with traditional fillings (икра – caviar, or селёдка – herring), fusion fillings (wild mixtures of, say, chicken and pineapple), or as a sweet with jam (варенье – *varene*).

Breakfast

Russian breakfasts (завтрак – *zavtrak*) are varied and include dairy products, pastries and other delicious treats made of dough, porridge of many kinds, eggs, as well as an assortment

Dining at the glorious venue of Peterhof palace

of smoked meats and fish, and sometimes cucumbers, tomatoes and other vegetables. Porridge (каша – *kasha*) is usually eaten with jam or sour cream (сметана – *smetana*). Cheese pancakes (сырники – *syrniki*) and blinys (блины) are also served with sour cream and jam. The dairy tray usually includes pot cheese (творог – *tvorog*), yoghurt (йогурт – *iogurt*) and lassi (кефир – *kefir*). In most restaurants or hotel cafés, you can find hard-boiled eggs (варёные яйца – *varyonye yaytsa*), omelette (омлет – *omlet*) or fried eggs (яичница – *yaichnitsa*). There will always be an ample supply of bread, both white (булка – *bulka*) and dark (чёрный – *chyorny*).

Lunch and Supper

Russians have traditionally eaten their largest meal in the middle of the day. Lunch (обед – *obed*) usually consists of a starter (закуски – *zakuski*) and/or salad (салат – *salat*), soup (суп – *sup*), a main course (второе – *vtoroe*) and dessert (сладкое – *sladkoe*). The evening meal (ужин – *uzhin*) is often a much lighter accompaniment to tea, like open-faced sandwiches (бутерброд – *buterbrod*). Today the demands of work make the full three-course lunch an impossibility for many, and evenings are the time to enjoy a lavish meal with friends.

Sour cream and dill

Many Russian dishes are served with sour cream and sprinkled liberally with dill. If you wish your dish to be garnish-free, say 'No sour cream' (без сметаны – *bez smetany*) or 'No dill' (без укропа – *bez ukropa*).

Zakuski and Salads

The glory of the Russian table is the first course, the *zakuski* – salads, sliced smoked meats, smoked and salted fish, fresh and pickled vegetables, salted and marinated mushrooms, and puff pastries (пирожки – *pirozhki*) filled with meat, potatoes, mushrooms, sautéed cabbage or fish. If you'd like a light meal, try a few of these starters.

Russian salads can be very complex (with inventive names and a long list of ingredients), or very simple, made traditionally of cucumbers and tomatoes (or radishes) seasoned with dill and with a sour cream or oil dressing. The classic mixed salad (винегрет – *vinegret*) is made of beetroot, potatoes, carrots and pickles, dressed with oil, mayonnaise or sour cream. Almost every restaurant has a version of the Salad 'Olivier' (салат «Оливье»), made of

A modern take on a classic dish

potatoes, onions, pickles and thin strips of meat (chicken, tongue or beef), and dressed with mayonnaise.

Russians eat a lot of fish – smoked, pickled, salted or baked with vegetables – as a starter. Herring (селёдка – *selyodka*) is traditionally served with fresh onions and boiled potatoes, or buried under a rich salad of beetroot, potatoes, boiled egg and sour cream in the fancifully named 'herring under a fur coat' (селёдка под шубой – *selyodka pod shuboi*). You might also try fish in aspic (заливное из рыбы – *zalivnoe iz ryby*), usually served with horseradish.

Russian caviar comes from several kinds of sturgeon found in the Caspian Sea: the Beluga, Ossetra and Sevruga. A fourth kind of caviar comes from the sterlet, a young sturgeon that

Bliny and caviar

is now rare. This is imperial caviar and, should you find it (and can afford it), is golden-yellow, with large, flavourful grains. Malossol, the delicate bluish-grey, lightly salted Beluga caviar, is one of the most highly prized for its slightly sweet and subtle flavour. Ossetra is light brown in colour and has a stronger fish taste. Sevruga has grey eggs and a robust flavour. Red salmon roe (красная икра – *krasnaya ikra*) has large red grains with a strong and salty flavour. All are eaten on bread or toast covered only with a bit of soft butter. Pancakes (блины – *bliny*) are served as a starter with caviar (икра – *ikra*).

Veal or beef in aspic (холодец – *kholdets*) is also served with horseradish as a starter, often with an assortment of smoked sausages (колбаса – *kolbasa*) and smoked meats (копченье – *kopchene*). For a hot starter, you could try a dish called Julienne (жюльен – *zhyulen*), a little pot of sliced mushrooms served in a white sauce topped with cheese and served bubbling hot from the oven.

Soups

Russians of the old school believe that a meal is not a meal without a bowl of soup. You can try borscht (борщ), a Ukrainian soup that Russians have adopted and claimed as their own. This beetroot soup can be made with fresh cabbage or sauerkraut, mushrooms, beef, or even prunes. It is traditionally served with hot rolls called *pampushki* (пампушки), which are drizzled with garlic sauce. Another hearty soup is *pokhlyobki* (похлёбки), made from meat, poultry or fish with onions, potatoes and carrots, or *solyanka* (солянка), a slightly sour soup made of mushrooms, fish or meat seasoned with pickles, olives, capers and lemons and topped with sour cream.

Lighter soups include mushroom (грибной – *gribnoy*), made with aromatic field mushrooms, most commonly porcini; a light fish soup (уха – *ukha*) seasoned with potatoes, carrots and onions; or clear chicken soups (куриная лапша – *kurinaya lapsha*). For good peasant fare, try the cabbage soup (щи – *shchi*), made with fresh cabbage or sauerkraut, broth and seasoned with a dollop of sour cream.

In the summer, Russians enjoy *okroshka* (окрошка), an unusual soup made of *kvas* (квас), a mildly alcoholic drink made from black bread, ladled over diced vegetables, or a clear beetroot soup (свекольник – *svekolnik*) that is ladled over a salad of potatoes, cucumbers and radishes, dressed with sour cream and seasoned with dill or parsley.

Main Dishes

For a classic Russian main course, try *pelmeni* (пельмени), the Russian version of ravioli, made of a mixture of pork,

Beef Stroganov

Beef Stroganov was named after Count Alexander Stroganov, who was a governor general in the south of Russia and lived in Odessa. Wealthy and luxury-loving, as well as generous, he held 'open houses' where anyone who was well dressed and mannered could stop in for lunch. For these luncheons, the count asked his chefs to invent a meat dish that could be easily served and eaten. The chefs came up with a dish that was something of a hybrid of French and Russian cuisine: tiny strips of beef served in a tomato and sour cream sauce. The dish was first popularised in Odessa cookbooks, where it was called Beef à la Stroganoff, and then was adapted throughout the empire – and eventually the world.

beef and/or lamb wrapped in pasta dough. Upscale restaurants experiment with non-traditional fillings, like venison, rabbit or pumpkin.

For memories of imperial Russia, try Beef Stroganov in a rich sour cream sauce, or other pre-revolutionary dishes made of venison, boar, suckling pig, goose or duck, usually baked with apples or cabbage and served with a tart berry sauce. Russians are also proud of their cutlets (котлеты – *kotlety*), made of virtually any meat or combination, and fried until they are crisp on the outside but succulent on the inside.

In most restaurants you order garnishes (гарнир – *garner*) separately, from a choice that includes vegetables (овощи – *ovoshchi*), French fries (картофель фри – *kartofelfri*), mashed potatoes (картофельное пюре – *kartofelnoe pyure*) or buckwheat oats (гречневая каша – *grechnevaya kasha*).

Drinks and Sweets

At table Russians drink mineral water, soda or a fruit drink: *mors* (морс), a refreshing drink made of fresh berries mixed with sugar and water, or juice (сок – *sok*). If you decide to try vodka with your starter, be sure to drink the Russian way: after a sip of vodka – or shot glass, depending on your stamina – immediately take a bite of food and a gulp of water or fruit drink. If you can't handle vodka, there are plenty of good Russian and imported wines to accompany your meals. Be sure to say whether you want dry (сухое – *sukhoe*) or sweet (сладкое – *sladkoe*). Russian sparkling wine (шампанское – *shampanskoe*) is also surprisingly good, although the best brut (брют) can be hard to find. You might also try some of the older pre-revolutionary drinks that are being revived, such as *sbiten'* (сбитень), a hot fermented drink made of honey and spices, and *medovukha* (медовуха), a spiced honey wine.

Meals end with tea (чай – *chay*), usually with lemon and sugar, or coffee (кофе – *kofe*), and a pastry (пирожное –

Many meals end with tea

pirozhenoe) or cake (торт – *tort*). You should also try Russian ice cream (мороженое – *morozhenoe*), which is deliciously rich and creamy, and usually served with berries or jam. A traditional sweet is *kisel* (кисель), a soft jelly made of fruits and thickened with cornflour.

Vegetarian Cuisine

Vegetarians had a hard time in Soviet Russia, but today most menus offer vegetarian dishes, often pastas or grilled vegetables, and all the better restaurants provide a separate menu (постное меню – *postnoe menyu*) that includes no meat, fish or dairy products during the four religious fasts. During the rest of the year, identify yourself as a vegetarian (вегетарианец – *vegetarianets*) and ask the serving staff for help. There is usually an ample selection of salads and vegetable soups (овощной суп-пюре – *ovoshchnoy sup-pyure*), as well as potato-filled dumplings (вареники с катофелем

– *vareniki s kartofelem*) and dozens of dishes made with mushrooms and grains. The cuisines from the Caucasus offer many vegetarian dishes, as do the many pizza cafés and Italian restaurants.

To Help You Order…

Is there a table free?	Есть свободный столик?	**Est svobodny stolik?**
I'd like…	Мне…	**Mne…**
waiter/menu	официант/меню	**ofitsiant/menyu**
The bill, please	Посчитайте, пожалуйста	**Poschitayte, pozhaluysta**
bread	хлеб	**khleb**
butter	масло	**maslo**
coffee	кофе	**kofe**
dessert	сладкое	**sladkoe**
fish	рыба	**ryba**
fruit	фрукты	**frukti**
ice cream	мороженое	**morozhenoe**
meat	мясо	**myaso**
milk	молоко	**moloko**
pepper	перец	**perets**
potatoes	картофель	**kartofel**
rice	рис	**ris**
salad	салат	**salat**
salt	соль	**sol**
sandwich	бутерброд	**buterbrod**
soup	суп	**sup**
sugar	сахар	**sakhar**
wine	вино	**vino**

… and Read the Menu

porridge	каша	**kasha**
frankfurter	сосиска	**sosiska**

smoked/boiled sausage	копчёная/варёная колбаса	**kopchyonaya/vary- onaya kolbasa**
pancake/bliny	блины	**bliny**
stuffed bliny	блинчики	**blinchiki**
potato salad	салат «Столичный»	**salat 'Stolichny'**
green salad	зелёный салат	**zelyony salat**
fresh vegetables	свежие овощи	**svezhie ovoshchi**
assorted fish/ smoked meats	рыбное/мясное ассорти	**rybnoe/myasnoe assorti**
marinated mushrooms	маринованные грибы	**marinovannye griby**
beef/veal	говядина/ телятина	**govyadina/ telyatina**
pork	свинина	**svinina**
cutlets	котлеты	**kotlety**
lamb	баранина	**baranina**
venison	оленина	**olenina**
chicken	курица/цыплёнок	**kuritsa/tsyplyonok**
duck	утка	**utka**
goose	гусь	**gus**
cod	треска	**treska**
trout	форель	**forel**
sturgeon	осетрина	**osetrina**
young sturgeon	стерлядь	**sterlyad**
crayfish	раки	**raki**
shrimp	креветки	**krevetki**
grilled	на гриле	**na grile**
fresh (pl)	свежие	**svezhie**
smoked (pl)	копчёные	**kopchyonye**
fried/sautéed (pl)	жареные	**zharenye**
baked/roasted (pl)	тушёные	**tushyonye**
stuffed (pl)	фаршированные	**farshirovannye**
pastry	пирожное	**pirozhnoe**

HANDY TRAVEL TIPS

An A–Z Summary of Practical Information

A

ACCOMMODATION

St Petersburg has a wide range of accommodation, from 'mini-hotels' – small private hotels made out of one or more renovated communal apartments – to Soviet-era monster hotels (now refurbished for the modern tourist) to some of the best five-star hotels in the world. Prices range from US$30 off season in a modest mini-hotel to out-of-the-stratosphere for the de luxe offerings. Another option is a serviced apartment, which includes registration, maid service and usually cable TV and either WiFi or high-speed internet. They can be found on <www.waytorussia.net>, or through private firms, such as <www.nevskyinn.ru> or <www.nevsky88.com>.

Virtually all hotels provide concierge services, such as obtaining theatre tickets and arranging for guides, cars and drivers, and include a buffet breakfast as part of the price of the room.

I'd like a single/ double room	Мне, пожалуйста, одноместный/ двухместный номер. **Mne, pozhaluysta, odnomestny/ dvukhmestny nomer.**
What's the rate per night?	Сколько стоит номер за одни сутки? **Skolko stoit nomer za odni sutki?**
My lamp/television doesn't work.	Лампа/телевизор не работает. **Lampa/televisor ne rabotaet.**

ADDRESSES

Russian addresses require a bit of deciphering. An address with a slash in the number, such as Nevsky 24/1, means that it is a corner building, number 24 on the main street and number 1 on the perpendicular street. Several buildings can share the same house number but are distinguished by an additional building (строение –

stroenie) or block (корпус – *korpus*) number. For example, an address might be Nevsky 24, stroenie 4.

boulevard	бульвар	**bulvar**
bridge	мост	**most**
embankment (river)	набережная	**naberezhnaya**
lane	переулок	**pereulok**
avenue	проспект	**prospekt**
square	площадь	**ploshchad**
highway	шоссе	**shosse**
street	улица	**ulitsa**

AIRPORTS

The main international airport in St Petersburg is Pulkovo 2, located about 17km (11 miles) to the south of the city. Pulkovo 1, about 10 minutes away, serves domestic flights and flights to the former Soviet republics. The airport information number is 812-704 3444.

For first-time visitors, it is best to use the airport transfer services provided by your hotel (about US$40) or one of the official taxis (about US$60) ordered from a booth in the arrivals hall. Don't use one of the taxi drivers who approach you in the terminal. If you feel adventurous and don't have much baggage, you can take Bus 13 (from Pulkovo 2) to Moskovskaya metro station, or one of the many minibuses (маршрутное такси – *marshrutnoe taksi*) to the city centre.

B

BRIDGES

One of the most charming sights of St Petersburg is the opening of the bridges over the Neva – unless you are on the wrong side of the river. Be aware that the bridges open from about 12.30am–6am from April to November.

BUDGETING FOR YOUR TRIP

St Petersburg can be expensive in and around the five-star hotels and during White Nights, when prices go up by about 30 percent.

Entertainment. If you don't opt for the best box seats, theatre and concert tickets are US$10–20, and opera and ballet up to US$50.

Meals. Dinner for two (starter, main and drinks) in one of the many modest restaurants and cafés can be had for US$50 or less, but expect to pay twice that in one of the more elegant eateries.

Museums. A two-tiered pricing system with higher entrance for foreigners, at around US$11, operates in many of the city's museums. A full day at the Hermitage costs about US$18.

Refreshments. Coffee and a snack at one of the city's ubiquitous coffee shops costs about US$7–10, but a soft drink and pastry from a kiosk is about US$5.

Transport. Taxis around the city are usually under US$10, even through car services. A car and driver cost US$15–100 an hour (depending on the class of car), but one ride on the metro (regardless of distance) is less than US$1.

C

CAR HIRE

If your Russian is good, your insurance is up to date and your nerves are made of steel, you might consider renting a car in St Petersburg (see DRIVING). You need to have an International Driver's Licence, a credit card and, with most agencies, be over 25 years old. Biracs <www.biracs.ru> has good rates, as does Cars in Time <www.rent-cars.ru> or Pulkowo Rent-a-Car <www.pulkoworent.ru> with a branch at the airport. A much safer and more pleasant alternative is to hire a car with a driver. Most hotels arrange services. The taxi service Fortuna (tel: 812-322 0000) provides a driver (Russian-speaking) for about US$25 for 24 hours. You might also ask for recommendations on the forum at <www.petersburgcity.com>, <www.expat.ru> or <www.redtape.ru>.

Tour guides (see GUIDES AND TOURS) often know drivers and can provide a 'package' service for you.

I'd like to rent a car.	Я хочу взять машину напрокат.
	Ya khochu vzyat mashinu na prokat.
with a driver/	с водителем/без водителя
without a driver	**s voditelem/bez voditelya**
tomorrow	на завтра
	na zavtra
for one day/week	на один день/на неделю
	na odin den/na nedelyu

CLIMATE

St Petersburg's climate is tempered by the proximity of the sea, so although the temperatures might be higher than inland cities at the same latitude, the damp makes it feel much colder. Spring arrives in April or May, summers are warm but rarely scorching hot, by late August temperatures become autumnal, and the first snow can fall in October or November. December until March is usually cold and snowy. In the height of the summer White Nights the sun virtually never sets – but in the depth of winter there are only about six hours of pallid light. Over the last decade the weather has been wildly unpredictable, so be prepared for a variety of temperatures and rainfall.

	J	F	M	A	M	J	J	A	S	O	N	D
min												
°C	-8	-8	-5	1	7	12	14	13	8	4	-2	-6
°F	18	18	24	34	44	53	58	55	47	39	28	22
max												
°C	-4	-4	2	9	15	20	22	20	14	8	1	-2
°F	25	25	36	48	60	68	72	68	58	47	34	28

CLOTHING

Young and wealthy Russians are very fashion-conscious, but average residents are not. You will rarely need formal dress; people attend the opera straight from work, so unless you want to dress up, you don't need to. In the summer, be sure to bring a sweater and rainwear (including waterproof shoes). In winter, you will need to bring a heavy coat or down jacket, hat, gloves and scarf, and boots that grip snow and ice.

Buildings, however, tend to be overheated, so you are unlikely to need heavy sweaters inside. Almost all museums, restaurants and businesses insist that you leave outerwear in the cloakroom (гардероб – *garderob*) as soon as you enter the building (tipping is not required).

The city streets are rarely well cleaned, which means they are coated with a thick layer of ice in the winter and an equally thick layer of mud at all other times of the year. Be sure to bring comfortable low-heeled shoes or boots that can withstand ice, mud, slush and puddles.

CONSULATES

Australia: Italyanskaya ulitsa 1, tel: 812-325 7333
Canada: Malodetskoselsky prospekt 32, tel: 812-325 8448
UK: Ploshchad Proletarskoy diktatury 5, tel: 812-320 3200
US: Furshtatskaya ulitsa 15, tel: 812-331 2600

Where is the US/UK embassy?	Где американское/британское консольство? **Gde amerikanskoe/britanskoe konsolstvo?**
I want to speak with my consul.	Я хочу поговорить с моим консулом. **Ya khochu pogovorit s moim konsulom.**

CRIME AND SAFETY

St Petersburg is probably safer than most major European cities. You should take the normal precautions for any large city: put valuables in the hotel safe, don't carry large amounts of cash, and beware of pickpockets in crowded places (including the metro) or markets. Avoid the parks at night. Change money in marked change booths only, and be sure to count the cash that you take from the sliding drawer (there is a scam in which one banknote gets stuck in the drawer thanks to a bit of glue). Do not fall for another scam in which a large wad of bills is 'dropped' in the street; if you pick it up, the person who 'dropped it' will return and insist the sum was twice what you picked up.

Nationalism and racism are becoming a serious problem. Skinheads (recognisable by their shaved heads, black or military-style clothing) prey on blacks, Asians and dark-skinned people. Avoid groups of them, particularly at night on the metro.

If you are robbed, you'll need to go to the militia (police) precinct to file a report and get a *spravka*, an official document registering the crime (which you'll need for the insurance settlement). Your hotel or the tourist information office (see TOURIST INFORMATION) can assist you.

I've been robbed.	Меня ограбили. **Menya ograbili.**
My passport/visa was stolen.	Украли мой паспорт/мою визу. **Ukrali moy pasport/moyu visu.**
I want to file a complaint with the police.	Я хочу написать заявление в милицию. **Ya khochu zayavlenie napisat v militsiyu.**
I need a document from the militia about the crime for my insurance.	Чтобы получить страховку, мне нужна справка из милиции. **Chtoby poluchit strakhovku, mne nuzhna spravka iz militsii.**

CUSTOMS AND ENTRY REQUIREMENTS

Visas. All visitors to Russia must have a visa and a passport valid for six months after departure with at least two free pages for the visa and stamps. If you arrange your trip through an agency as part of a group or individual tour, the agency will handle all the visa formalities for you. If you are arranging your own travel, you will have to book the hotel and return ticket before applying for the visa. You will need to send a completed application form (available through tour agencies, the consulate or online) with a passport-size photograph stapled in the space provided; a standard tourist confirmation (from the travel agency or hotels) and voucher (proof of payment); a cover letter with the applicant's name, arrival and departure dates, flight or train numbers, and itinerary within the country; your passport; and a cheque to cover the processing fees.

Full instructions, addresses and fees are listed on Russian embassy sites in each country. Tourist visas are issued for up to one month and cannot be extended. Although tourist visas can be processed within one day, it's best to allow several weeks. You can also use the services of companies such as Way to Russia <www.waytorussia.net>, which provides visa support and registration.

When you arrive in the country, you must fill out a migration card. Airlines provide them on board, and attendants help you fill them out. You must be registered during your stay. This is arranged by hotels or the inviting agency (including visa and tour companies and most apartment rental agencies). A receipt proves legal registration.

Customs. You must also fill out a customs declaration for any cash and travellers' cheques over US$10,000. In this case, use the Red Channel at the airport so that the customs officer can stamp your declaration. When you leave, you will also have to fill out a new form if you are taking out more than US$3,000. You are not allowed to take out more money than you brought in without a stamped document from the bank (if you withdrew cash) or other certification that you received the money legally. Receipts from ATMs are not valid proof.

You can bring into the country 2 litres of alcohol, 50 cigars or 200 cigarettes, and baggage up to 35kg (77lbs) without paying a duty fee.

You may take out of the country only 250g (0.6lbs) of black caviar per person in factory-sealed jars and 'a reasonable amount' of red caviar, also in factory-sealed jars. You may not take out any antiques over 50 years old or fine art without special permission from the Ministry of Culture. Permission can be arranged in the finer galleries and shops, although it takes at least five days (and usually longer). It is a good idea to keep receipts for any expensive souvenirs.

Documents. By the time you get to your hotel, you will have a little packet of documents: visa, migration card, passport, registration receipt and possibly customs form. It's a good idea to make copies of all these documents in your hotel and leave them in your room or in the hotel safe. You should carry your passport, visa, registration receipt and migration card with you at all times; it's also a good idea to carry a card with your hotel name and address in case you get lost. If your documents are lost or stolen, you will have to go to a police precinct to get an official document of theft/loss and to your consulate for a new passport and assistance replacing your Russian documents.

I've nothing to declare.	Мне нечего декларировать.
	Mne nechevo deklarirovat.
It's for my personal use.	Это для личного пользования.
	Eto dlya lichnovo polzovaniya.

D

DISABLED TRAVELLERS

St Petersburg is not a disabled-person friendly city. Some of the Western-run and owned hotels, like the Petro Palace, Radisson SAS and Kempinski, have wheelchair-accessible rooms and public spaces. A few of the main museums, like the Hermitage, are barrier-free.

Since tourists in wheelchairs will need to be carried upstairs, it is recommended to bring a lighter manual chair. Up-to-date information on issues of interest to disabled people can be found on the website of the organisation Perspektiva <www.perspektiva-inva.ru>.

DRIVING

St Petersburg is a difficult city for drivers: the traffic is getting worse every day, the roads are badly maintained but seem to be constantly under construction; the drivers are reckless and aggressive. Not surprisingly, Russia's rate of fatal road accidents is about 10 times higher than Britain's. Should you wish to take the challenge, you should have an international licence, know that traffic drives on the right, seat belts are mandatory, and the speed limit within cities is 60kph (38mph), and up to 100kph (62mph) on highways out of the city, unless otherwise marked. Parking is only allowed where marked (P), though few drivers follow this law. Left turns are not usually allowed unless marked or indicated with an arrow on the traffic light.

Petrol stations can be found throughout the city, often with shops, car washes and cafés. Lukoil, BP and other branded stations provide pump service. At other stations you pay first and then fill the tank yourself. Most provide 92-, 95- and 98-octane and diesel fuel.

E

ELECTRICITY

Russia has 200V/50Hz AC, with European-style round two-pin sockets. However, Russian sockets are narrower than European standard pins; ask the concierge or reception desk for an adaptor (переходник – *perekhodnik*).

EMERGENCIES

There are four emergency numbers that are standard for all of Russia, although the operators only speak Russian:

Fire **01**   Police **02**   Ambulance **03**   Gas **04**

Russians are very responsive to someone in need, be it a minor problem (getting lost, breaking a shoe) or a major emergency (being robbed, becoming ill). If you are in trouble, walk up to someone and start talking; the person will try to find an English speaker or help.

Help!	Помогите!	**Pomogite!**
Police!	Милиция!	**Militsiya!**
Call an ambulance!	Позвоните в скорую помощь!	
	Pozvonite v skoruyu pomoshch!	
I'm/we're lost!	Я/мы заблудил(ся)/(ась)/(ись)!	
	Ya/my zabludilsya/zabludilas/zabludilis	
	(masculine singular/feminine singular/plural).	

G

GAY AND LESBIAN TRAVELLERS

Homosexuality was a crime in Soviet times and is still condemned by the Russian Orthodox Church and many Russians. Skinheads and religious groups have targeted some gay clubs in St Petersburg and have attacked clients when they leave, and the police are sometimes indifferent (or worse) to complaints from gays and lesbians. However, attitudes are changing, and there is a lively gay club scene. The site <www.gay.ru> has an extensive English-language section with listings for bars, clubs, guides and other entertainment. The Krilija Centre <www.krilija.ru> has a gay tourist agency serving St Petersburg.

GETTING THERE (See also AIRPORTS)

By air. Although there are flights daily from nearly 40 European cities, passengers from North America, Australia and New Zealand will have a stopover.

By ship. Ferries arrive from Sweden, Germany, Finland and Estonia. Most trips take about 14 hours overnight.

By rail. Trains from the Baltic and Eastern European countries take between 15 and 37 hours. Be aware that you'll need a transit visa, obtained in advance, to pass through Belarus. Trains from the west arrive at Vitebsky Station. Three trains leave Helsinki every day; they take from about six to eight hours and arrive at Ladozhsky Station. From the east, trains from Beijing and Vladivostok make the week-long trip several times a week.

GUIDES AND TOURS

Many companies provide package tours to St Petersburg that include visa, hotel, meals and tours. For independent travellers, city tours and a variety of suburban palace tours are run every day in English by the trustworthy and competent Eclectica-Guide. Their kiosk is at the southeast corner of Gostiny Dvor (tel: 812-710 5529; <www.eclectica-guide.ru>). They can also arrange individual tours.

Peter's Walking Tours run interesting tours around the city, including a bicycle tour on Sunday mornings. For most of them, you just turn up at the meeting point a few minutes before the tour starts. A list of tours can be found at <www.peterswalk.com>.

Another option is a freelance guide. Check the forums at <www.expat.ru>, <www.redtape.ru> or <www.waytorussia.net>. They charge about US$15/hour and can often provide a car and driver at extra cost. Some museums have English-speaking guides; book in advance.

We'd like an English-speaking guide/ an English interpreter.	Нам нужен англоязычный экскурсовод/переводчик. **Nam nuzhen angloyazychny ekskursovod/perevodchik.**
Do you have tours in English?	У вас есть экскурсия на английском? **U vas est ekskursiya na angliyskom?**

H

HEALTH AND MEDICAL CARE

No vaccinations are compulsory for St Petersburg and Russia, and the only city-specific health risk is the tap water, which you should not drink. Inexpensive mineral water (минеральная вода – *mineralnaya voda*) is available virtually everywhere.

Bring all necessary prescription drugs and have medical insurance that covers you abroad and includes medical evacuation. Russian health care is underfinanced and patchy; in case of illness, seek help at a clinic catering to foreigners. Bring insurance forms with you; in most cases you will have to pay for the services and be reimbursed when you return home. Two clinics that provide 24/7 services, including dentistry, with English-speaking and trained physicians, are:

American Medical Clinic, Nab. reki Moiki 78, tel: 812-740 2090.

MEDEM International Clinic and Hospital, Ulitsa Marata 6, tel: 812-336 3333.

Lensmasters Glasses and Contact Lenses provides a one-hour service with several shops at city shopping centres, including Ramstore Udelny (tel: 812-336 5449; <www.lensmaster.ru>).

Where's the nearest (all-night) pharmacy?	Где ближайшая (круглосуточная) аптека?	**Gde blizhayshaya (kruglosutochnaya) apteka?**
I need a doctor/ dentist.	Мне нужен врач/зубной врач.	**Mne nuzhen vrach/zubnoy vrach.**
an ambulance	скорая помощь	**skoraya pomoshch**
a hospital	больница	**bolnitsa**
I have a stomach/ toothache.	У меня болит желудок/зуб.	**U menya bolit zheludok/zub.**
I have a fever.	У меня температура.	**U menya temperatura.**

Pharmacies. These are plentiful and sell many common over-the-counter drugs, contact-lens solutions and standard chemist's sundries. There are all-night pharmacies in every district; look for the number '24' or ask at your hotel. 36.6 is a good Western-style pharmacy chain, and Arbat Prestizh is a chain selling beauty supplies and toiletries.

HOLIDAYS

Russian state holidays are:
1–7 January New Year and Orthodox Christmas
23 February Defenders of the Homeland Day
8 March International Women's Day
1 May Spring and Labour Holiday
9 May Victory Day
12 June Russia Day
4 November People's Unity Day

When holidays fall on Tuesday or Thursday, Monday or Friday are usually days off, with the Saturday after the holiday a working day. Note that embassies are closed on Russian and national holidays. See the Calendar of Events *(see page 95)* for information on festivals and Church holidays.

L

LANGUAGE

St Petersburg is trying to become more tourist-friendly, with signs, museum notes and even menus in English, but basic familiarity with the Cyrillic alphabet is strongly recommended.

In this guide, we have used the simplified system of transliteration provided below. Note that many male Russian names and adjectives end in -ой, -ий or -ый, which we transliterate as 'y'. In some cases, letters are transliterated as pronounced, such as the endings -oro, -ero (-evo, -ovo), and some names, like Tchaikovsky or Gorbachev, are given in the form that has become standard in English. Don't worry about soft and hard sounds; if you can hit most of the consonants in a word, people will understand you.

Russian	Transliteration	English Example
А а	a	a in father
Б б	b	b in book
В в	v	v in very
Г г	g	g in good
Д д	d	d in day
Е е	e (ye when first letter in a word)	ye in yet (note that words like 'lobnoe' are pronounced lob-noi-ye)
Ё ё	yo	yo in yonder
Ж ж	zh	s in pleasure or composure
З з	z	z in zoo
И и	i	ee in meet
Й й	y	y in boy
К к	k	k in kite
Л л	l	l in lamp
М м	m	m in map
Н н	n	n in not
О о	o	o in pot
П п	p	p in pet
Р р	r	r in restaurant (rolled r)
С с	s	s in sound
Т т	t	t in tip
У у	u	oo in hoot
Ф ф	f	f in face
Х х	kh	ch in Channukah (a guttural kh)
Ц ц	ts	ts in sits
Ч ч	ch	ch in chip
Ш ш	sh	sh in shut
Щ щ	shch	shch in fresh cheese

Ъ ъ		Placed after a consonant, this keeps the sound hard
Ы ы	y	i in ill
Ь ь		Placed after a consonant, this makes the sound palletised (soft)
Э э	e	e in extra
Ю ю	yu	u in use
Я я	ya	ya in yard

Hello	Здравствуйте	**Zdravstvuyte**
Good morning	Доброе утро	**Dobroe utro**
Good day/evening	Добрый день/ вечер	**Dobry den/ vecher**
Goodbye	До свидания	**Do svidaniya**
Please	Пожалуйста	**Pozhaluysta**
Thank you	Спасибо	**Spasibo**
Help!	Помогите!	**Pomogite!**
Good/bad	Хорошо/плохо	**Khorosho/plokho**
I don't speak Russian	Я не говорю по-русски	**Ya ne govoryu po-russki**
I don't understand	Я не понимаю	**Ya ne ponimayu**
Toilet W/M	Туалет Ж/М	**Tualet Zh/M**
Danger	Опасно	**Opasno**
Open/closed	Открыто/закрыто	**Otkryto/zakryto**
Where/when/how/ who/why	Где/когда/как/ кто/почему	**Gde/kogda/kak/ kto/pochemu**
Start/continuation of exhibition	Начало/ продолжение осмотра	**Nachalo/ prodolzhenie osmotra**
Shoe covers	Бахилы	**Bakhili**
Entrance/exit	Вход/выход	**Vkhod/vykhod**
Cashier/ticket office	Касса	**Kassa**

M

MAPS

Good maps in Russian and English are available at tourist centres (see TOURIST INFORMATION), in bookshops, in many museums and in virtually all hotels.

MEDIA

Most hotels provide cable television with a full array of English-language news and entertainment channels. News-stands in major hotels as well as foreign-owned supermarkets have current English-language magazines and the *International Herald Tribune*.

The *St Petersburg Times* (<www.sptimes.ru>) is published twice a week and is the main source for local news and entertainment listings. The glossy monthly *Pulse* (<www.pulse.ru>) provides feature stories and cultural listings, as does *Where*, which can be found in hotels and many restaurants.

Some entertainment listings and news can be found in the monthly *Neva News* (<www.nevanews.com>). Several other official and unofficial (i.e. commercial) guides can be found around the city. They are published quarterly, with cultural listings and feature articles.

MONEY

The currency in Russia is the rouble, which consists of 100 kopeks. There are bills in denominations of 10, 50, 100, 500, 1,000 and 5,000, and coins of one, five, 10 and 50 kopeks, as well as one, two, five and 10 roubles.

Travellers' cheques can usually only be cashed or used in major hotels or some banks. The American Express office is located at Ulitsa Malaya Morskaya 23 (tel: 812-326 4500). Major credit cards are accepted at most hotels and many stores, and an increasing number of restaurants.

Cash machines/ATMs (банкомат – *bankomat*) can be found throughout the city and are considered secure these days, although be sure to take the usual safety precautions at street terminals. Only exchange money at official exchange offices (обмен – *obmen*), in banks or hotels.

I'd like to exchange money.	Я хочу обменять деньги. **Ya khochu obmenyat dengi.**
Do you accept credit cards?	Вы принимаете кредитные карты? **Vy prinimaete kreditnye karty?**
Can I cash travellers' cheques?	Можно обналичить дорожные чеки? **Mozhno obnalichit dorozhnye cheki?**

O

OPENING TIMES

There are no standard opening and closing times. Banks and state offices open their doors at about 8.30am and close at 6 or 7pm, often with an hour off for lunch. Most shops open around 10 or 11am and close at 8 to 10pm; a few still close for lunch. Restaurants often stay open until the last client has left, and there are hundreds of 24-hour kiosks, food shops, cafés and clubs. Each museum has its own idiosyncratic hours, and is usually closed one or two days a week, plus one additional 'cleaning' day per month. Check individual listings carefully. Museums stop selling entry tickets an hour before closing.

P

PHOTOGRAPHY

There are hundreds of photographic equipment, film and digital processing shops all over the city. Note that it is illegal to take photographs of any military installation or inside the metro (although the latter is rarely enforced), and the guards at many private buildings will prevent you from taking pictures for security reasons. When in doubt, ask.

May we take a picture of this/of you?	Можно это/вас сфотографировать? **Mozhno eto/vas sfotografirovat?**
I'd like to develop and print this film.	Мне нужно проявить плёнку и напечатать фотокарточки. **Mne nuzhno proyavit plyonku i napechatat fotokartochki.**

POLICE

The local police (милиция – *militsiya*) often stop pedestrians for document checks. Hand them your documents but not your purse or wallet (money has been known to disappear during the check). Despite their patchy reputation, most Russian police officers try their best to be helpful and kind if you're lost or in trouble (though few speak English). Your hotel or the tourist centre (see TOURIST INFORMATION) can provide assistance.

Where's the nearest police station?	Где ближайшее отделение милиции? **Gde blizhayshee otdelenie militsii?**

POST OFFICE

The Russian postal system (почта – *pochta*) is still slow, though most letters, parcels and postcards eventually reach their destination. Cards and letters can usually be posted from your hotel. Express service should be handled by one of the international courier companies operating in the city: DHL (tel: 812-326 6400; <www.dhl.ru>) or TNT Express (tel: 812-718 3439; <www.tnt.ru>).

PUBLIC TRANSPORT

St Petersburg has an excellent and cheap public transport system. With traffic worsening, the fastest way to get anywhere is underground.

Metro. The stations are marked with a red 'M'. Inside the station, buy tokens at the ticket office (or through machines), pop one into the turnstile, and hop on the fast-moving escalator.

Trams, trolleys and buses. Hop on and pay the fare to the conductor, who somehow manages to make the rounds between stops. In mini-buses (маршрутки – *marshrutki*) you pay the driver directly.

Taxis. You'll find these clustered around hotels and a few main squares. It is difficult to catch a cab cruising the streets. However, if you stand on the road and hold your hand out, in a few minutes 'private cab drivers' (i.e. people moonlighting in their own cars) will undoubtedly stop. Despite the apparent danger, this is the standard way to get around the city. The only safety precaution is avoiding any car with one or more additional passengers. State your destination and your price (usually around 200 roubles for a short distance, up to 500 or more for a long distance or at night) and hop in.

Where can I get a taxi?	Где можно найти такси? **Gde mozhno nayti taksi?**
What's the fare to...?	Сколько стоит проезд до...? **Skolko stoit proezd do...?**
Where is the nearest bus stop/ metro station?	Где ближайшая остановка автобуса/станция метро? **Gde blizhaishaya ostanovka avtobusa/stantsiya metro?**
Will you tell me when to get off?	Вы подскажете, когда мне выходить? **Vy podskazhete, kogda mne vykhodit?**
What's the next stop/station?	Какая следующая остановка/станция? **Kakaya sleduyushchaya ostanovka/stantsiya?**

R

RELIGION

The main religion in Russia is the Russian Orthodox Church, and almost all of the churches that beacme museums, concert halls, offices or warehouses during the Soviet years have been returned to the Church. Because the Soviet authorities plundered the rich interiors, many churches that are beautiful on the outside have only a few icons against whitewashed walls inside. Some churches are only open for services (usually 9am and 5pm).

Services in English are held at the Anglican Chaplaincy in St Catherine's Church (Malaya Konyushennaya 1–3; <www.anglican.ru>), the Roman Catholic Parish of St Catherine (Nevsky prospekt 32–34, tel: 812-571 6619), and the Sha'arei Shalom Progressive Jewish Community (7-aya Liniya 34; <www.freewebs.com/shaarei shalom>). Detailed information is listed in the Friday edition of the *St Petersburg Times*.

T

TELEPHONE

The country code for Russia is 7 and the city code for St Petersburg is 812. For local calls, public telephones can be found near and in metro stations. You can buy a phonecard (телефонная карта – *telefonnaya karta*) at a ticket office in denominations of 20 and 50 minutes.

To make an international call, dial 8 and wait for the dial tone to repeat, then 10, then the country and city codes and number.

International telephone fees in hotels are exorbitant, and it is much cheaper to buy a calling card (also called телефонная карта) from one of the mobile-phone centres or booths near every major intersection and metro station. Country codes: US and Canada: 1, UK: 44, Australia: 61, New Zealand: 64.

TIME ZONES

St Petersburg is GMT plus three hours. Daylight-saving time begins at 2am on the last Sunday in March and ends at 3am on the last Sunday in October.

TIPPING

Tipping is rather haphazard: expected but not mandatory. In restaurants and cafés, 10 percent is ample (if a service charge is not added to the bill). In bars and clubs, customers round up the cost of a drink. Taxi drivers and hotel staff expect tips for assisting with bags (50–100 roubles) and tour guides will also welcome a tip (200 roubles or more, if the service was excellent).

TOILETS

There are paid public toilets (usually blue plastic) by metro stations and in most public parks; public toilets can also be found in every mall and museum. Facilities in restaurants, cafés and bars are generally clean, but they may not always have toilet paper.

Where is the toilet?   Где здесь туалет?   **Gde zdes tualet?**

TOURIST INFORMATION

There are tourist centres on Palace Square (Dvortsovaya ploshchad 12) and at Ulitsa Sadovaya 14/52, which provide free maps, assistance and advice, and also have a wide variety of print materials for sale. Area maps can be found on stands outside most metro stations.

WEBSITES AND INTERNET CAFÉS

Websites. There are thousands of sites providing information about St Petersburg in English. For official information, see **www.**

petersburgcity.com. That site, as well as **www.gotorussia.com**, **www.redtape.ru** and **www.expat.ru** have helpful information and forums. The site **www.restoran.ru/spb** has an English version with fairly complete and updated restaurant listings and a reservation service.

Internet. Virtually all hotels have internet access (often WiFi, at least in the public areas), but if you need an internet café, there are plenty in the city centre that are open 24 hours. The best of them is Quo Vadis (Nevsky prospekt 76, entrance from Liteyny prospekt, tel: 812-333 0708), which has a café and a variety of business services. The chain Cafémax has opened up branches in St Petersburg (Nevsky prospekt 90/92, tel: 812-273 6655) and provides the basics for a young crowd.

Y

YOUTH HOSTELS

St Petersburg has a number of good youth hostels that provide visa support and registration (although some only provide registration if you arrive on their visa support). All provide laundry, internet, TV and decent security.

The oldest is the St Petersburg International Hostel (3-aya Sovetskaya ulitsa 28, tel: 812-329 8018), with doubles and dormitory rooms right in the city centre. Another popular one is the Puppet Theatre Hostel (Nekrasova ulitsa 14, tel: 812-272 5401), which offers rooms sleeping two, three or five people. The Sleep Cheap Hostel near the Fontanka (Mokhovaya ulitsa 18–32, tel: 812-273 5709) is smaller (two rooms sleeping eight each), but clean and friendly. The Nord Hostel is practically on Palace Square (Ulitsa Bolshaya Morskaya 10, tel: 812-571 0342), with two floors sleeping almost 50 travellers. The Hostel on Sadovaya (Sadovaya ulitsa 53, tel: 812-314 8357) sleeps 40 in rooms of two, three or five people.

Recommended Hotels

Although at present St Petersburg only derives about 2 percent of its income from tourism, the municipal authorities are determined to raise that figure. They have supported construction of new hotels of all classes and reconstructed 'mini-hotels' – former communal apartments that have been remodelled into small bed-and-breakfast establishments. Most of them are modest, but with en-suite bathrooms, round-the-clock kitchens and the standard array of concierge services. Some are 'walk-ups' with no lift – a fair price for a cheap bed and central location. At the other end of the price scale are some of the most sumptuous and luxurious hotels in the world. In between are hotels from the Soviet years that have been well refurbished and small boutique hotels set in historical buildings. In addition, there are serviced apartments which might suit travelling families.

Hotels and apartments can be booked directly online, through internet hotel agencies or tourist agencies. Prices are usually listed in roubles; sometimes they are listed in currency 'units', which the hotel itself defines. Be sure to enquire about the hotel exchange rate so you know the cost in your currency, and clarify whether the quoted price includes the 18 percent VAT.

The hotels listed are located in the city centre and provide visa support, internet, cable TV and breakfast, unless otherwise noted.

As a basic guide we have used the symbols below to indicate the price per night for a double room with bath. Note that prices rise about 20–30 percent during the peak season of White Nights.

$$$$	over US$300
$$$	US$200–300
$$	US$100–200
$	under US$100

NEAR THE ADMIRALTY AND HERMITAGE

Angleterre Hotel $$$$ *Ulitsa Bolshaya Morskaya 39, tel: 812-494 5666, fax: 812-494 5125, <www.angleterrehotel.com>.* Completely renovated by the Rocco Forte group, this elegant hotel has reclaimed its former luxury and comfort. Located across from St Isaac's Cathedral, next to its sister hotel the Astoria, it has almost 200 rooms, a good fitness centre with sauna and small pool, and several celebrated restaurants. Breakfast not included.

Astoria $$$$ *Ulitsa Bolshaya Morskaya 39, tel: 812-494 5666, fax: 812-494 5133, <www.thehotelastoria.com>.* The Astoria is one of the city's grand old hotels, built in 1912 and now fully renovated. The hotel has almost 200 rooms and every service one could want, including a full spa and 24-hour fitness centre, parquet floors, linen curtains and marble bathrooms. A truly eminent hotel in the city centre.

Central Inn $–$$ *Ulitsa Yakubovicha 2, Apt 14, tel: 812-571 4516, <www.central-inn.ru>.* This mini-hotel is right next to St Isaac's Cathedral, with 14 modern rooms, gym, sauna and pleasant café. It is rather modest, but the staff are extremely helpful and friendly. Visa support arranged through an affiliate agency.

Comfort Hotel $–$$ *Ulitsa Bolshaya Morskaya 25, tel: 812-570 6700, fax: 812-571 6724, <www.comfort-hotel.spb.ru>.* Located in the same building as the Herzen House, Comfort Hotel is accessible by lift, with 14 modern rooms and all the usual amenities.

Herzen House $$ *Ulitsa Bolshaya Morskaya 25, tel: 812-571 5098, fax: 812-314 6406, <www.herzenhotel.spb.ru>.* This pleasant mini-hotel is accessed by a lift and has 20 modern rooms with high ceilings and all the expected amenities. It is located a few blocks from the Hermitage in an area with plenty of restaurants and cafés.

Kempinski $$$$ *Nab. reki Moiki 22, tel: 812-335 9111, fax: 812-335 9190, <www.kempinski.com>.* The Kempinski has refurbished several old mansions into a luxurious hotel, with a spacious atrium, cosy wood-lined bar (with fireplace), wine-cellar bar and tea-room (with fireplace and live classical music). There are nearly 200 rooms, a fitness centre and a terrific café, the Bellevue Brasserie on the top floor with a fabulous 360-degree view of the city centre.

Moika 5 $$ *Nab. reki. Moika 5, tel: 812-601 0636, <www.hon. ru>*. Part of the Hotels on Nevsky group, Moika 5 is a bright little yellow house with 24 modern rooms of various classes (including split-level apartments with Jacuzzis and great views of the city). The public spaces have antique décor and there's a cheerful breakfast room.

Nevsky Inn 1 and 2 $ *Kirpichny pereulok 2, Apt 19, tel: 812-972 6873 and Malaya Morskaya 9, Apt 3, tel: 812-312 2686, <www. nevskyinn.ru>*. These small bed-and-breakfast inns (with seven and four rooms respectively) are extremely comfortable and cheap, with some of the most friendly and accommodating service in town. The Kirpichny pereulok address is a fourth-floor 'walk-up'; the smaller Inn is on the second floor. Both are located within two blocks of the Hermitage.

Old Vienna $$ *Ulitsa Malaya Morskaya 13 (entrance on Gorokhovaya ulitsa), tel: 812-312 9339, <www.vena.old-spb.ru>*. This boutique hotel was one of St Petersburg's most famous bohemian cafés at the turn of the 20th century. The fawn-green halls and rotunda café-breakfast room (where photos show St Petersburg's famous writers and artists dining just before the revolution) are decorated in *style moderne*. Each of the 14 rooms is dedicated to an artist or writer of the glorious Silver Age. This charming mini-hotel is located right in the city centre and worth the climb up three floors through a rather paint-chipped hall. No visa support.

Petro Palace Hotel $$$$ *Ulitsa Malaya Morskaya 14, tel: 812-571 2880, <www.petropalacehotel.com>*. The Petro Palace was once the mansion of Baron von Stahl and is now a rather elegant medium-sized hotel serving both business clients and tourists. The public spaces are filled with columns, marble and antiques, while the rooms are rather standard classical décor. The hotel has a large fitness centre (including pool and sauna). Breakfast not included with most rates.

Pushka Inn $$ *Nab. reki Moiki 14, tel: 812-312 0957, fax: 812-314 1055, <www.pushkainn.ru>*. Pushka Inn is located in a superbly refurbished 18th-century house, with public spaces that retain the building's original details and rooms that are simple and modern. It is a very cosy and inviting boutique hotel with 35 rooms, over-looking the Moika river in the city centre.

Renaissance Baltic $$$$ *Pochstamtskaya ulitsa 4, tel: 812-380 4000, fax: 812-380 4001, <www.renaissancehotels.com>.* This top-class modern hotel is three blocks from Nevsky prospekt, with a great deal of charm, from the airy atrium to the comfortable rooms, fitness centre, bars and restaurants. This is a quality hotel with a more personal touch.

Residence on Gorokhovaya $ *Gorokhovaya ulitsa 8, tel: 812-312 7377, <www.residencehotels.ru>.* This tiny, four-room mini-hotel is a 'walk-up' through rather run-down hallways, but its friendly staff, central location, modern rooms and excellent prices make it a good bargain.

Taleon Club Yeliseev Palace Hotel $$$$ *Nab. reki Moiki 59, tel: 812-324 9911, fax: 812-324 9957, <www.taleon.ru>.* If you have ever fantasised about spending a night in a palace, the Taleon is for you. The hotel is partly housed in a mansion that belonged to one of pre-revolutionary Russia's most successful businessmen. It has a marble-floored atrium and 29 over-the-top luxury rooms. The mansion itself houses a high-class casino and lounge, where you can play cards under Baccarat chandeliers or have a cognac in a wood-lined study with ancient stained-glass windows. The hotel, a member of the Leading Small Hotels of the World, has a spa, fit-ness centre and butler service.

MID-NEVSKY PROSPEKT

Antique Hotel Rachmaninov $$ *Kazanskaya ulitsa 5, tel: 812-571 7618, <www.hotelrachmaninov.com>.* Although this hotel is a third-floor 'walk-up', the stunning location (a few steps from Nevsky) and charming interior make the walk worthwhile. The halls are whitewashed brick, the rooms have pine furniture and wooden floors, and there is a bright lounge filled with antique furniture. The Rachmaninov Suite, where the composer lived as a child, has a tiny balcony with a fabulous view of the Kazan Cathedral and Nevsky prospekt.

Hotel Baskof $$ *Ulitsa Mayakovskovo 23/6 (entrance on Baskov pereulok), tel: 812-272 6493, <www.baskof-hotel.com>.* This 13-room mini-hotel has updated Silver Age décor (including a white ceramic corner stove in one of the rooms) with comfortable rooms and all the modern amenities. It is tucked away on a quiet street not far from the Fontanka and Nevsky prospekt.

Corinthia Nevskij Palace Hotel $$$$ *Nevsky prospekt 7, tel: 812-380 2001, fax: 812-380 1937, <www.corinthia.ru>.* This modern hotel provides traditional Western-standard comfort and services right on Nevsky prospekt. It has a good-sized fitness centre and a number of cafés and restaurants. Breakfast not included.

Dostoevsky $$$ *Vladimirsky prospekt 19, tel: 812-331 3200, fax: 812-331 321, <www.dostoevsky-hotel.ru>.* The Dostoevsky occupies the top floors of the handsome *style moderne* Vladimisky Passazh arcade, with plenty of cafés, bars, restaurants and shops close at hand, as well as a fitness centre and sauna. The public spaces have old-world, elegant décor, but its 200-plus rooms are modern.

Grand Hotel Europe $$$$ *Mikhailovskaya ulitsa 1/7, tel: 812-329 6000, fax: 812-329 6001, <www.gradhoteleurope.com>.* One of the world's best hotels, in recent years the Grand Hotel Europe has welcomed a pantheon of stars, from Queen Elizabeth and Bill Clinton to Sting and Jane Fonda. In the old days it was the hotel of choice for Lord and Lady Astor, not to mention Pyotr Tchaikovsky, George Bernard Shaw and Grigory Rasputin. Beautiful rooms, excellent service, six restaurants, fitness and business centres. Breakfast not included.

Helvetia Hotel & Suites $$$ *Ulitsa Marata 11, tel: 812-326 5353, fax: 812-326 2009, <www.helvetia-suites.ru>.* The Helvetia seems more like a friendly apartment building than a hotel, with guest entrances accessed through an open courtyard filled with flowers in the summertime. This nicely refurbished mansion has studio and family suites with kitchens, making it one of the best places for families in the city.

Radisson SAS $$$$ *Nevsky prospekt 49/2, tel: 812-322 5000, fax: 812-5001, <www.radissonsas.com>.* The people at Radisson SAS gutted a building dating from the 1730s, saving the façade but constructing a modern top-class hotel inside. It provides a high standard of service and amenities, including a fitness centre, right in the city centre.

Hotel Vesta $$ *Nevsky prospekt 90–92, tel: 812-272 1322, <www.vestahotel.spb.ru>.* Even though this hotel's address is on bustling Nevsky prospekt, it is actually tucked away from the crowds in a pleasant courtyard. The rooms are all modern European style and standard, although a few architectural details from past centuries remain in the public rooms. It caters to both tourists and business travellers.

NEAR PLOSHCHAD VOSTANIYA

Hotel Brothers Karamazov $$ *Ulitsa Sotsialisticheskaya 11-A, tel: 812-335 1185, <www.karamazovhotel.com>.* The Brothers Karamazov Hotel is located in the heart of Dostoevsky territory, about a 20-minute walk from Nevsky prospekt. The small hotel (28 rooms) has clean classical décor with some antiques in the public spaces and larger rooms. It caters to both tourists and business travellers, and has a restaurant that serves a full range of traditional Russian and European dishes.

Grand Hotel Emerald $$$$ *Suvorovsky prospekt 18, tel: 812-740 5002, fax: 812-740 5006, <www.grandhotelermerald.com>.* Although this newly built five-star hotel is a bit off the beaten track, it makes up for it with a luxurious interior, the largest rooms of the city's five-star hotels, a gym, full spa and lovely atrium lounge. The area (not far from the Alexander Nevsky Lavra) is a bit quieter than the bustle on Nevsky.

Oktyabrskaya Hotel $$ *Ligovsky prospekt 10, tel: 812-578 1515, fax: 812-315 7501, <www.oktober-hotel.spb.ru>.* This hotel dating from the mid-19th century has been refurbished from a rather stodgy Soviet hostelry into a modern hotel, with almost 500 rooms (each individually laid out) in two buildings. With all the usual amenities, several restaurants, bars and cafés and a fitness club, it is a good bargain in the city centre, although it may be a bit noisy.

Pushkinskaya 10 $–$$ *Ulitsa Pushinskaya 10, Apt 27, tel: 812-320 0983, fax: 812-320 0982, <www.hotel10.ru>.* This eight-room mini-hotel is a little hard to find, since the neighbours in this rather elegant building did not want any signposts to mar their entrance (look instead for the discreet sign on the doorbell). But this bed and breakfast (accessed by a lift) is a real bargain, with a cheery kitchen, sauna and rooms in different styles, from modern to antique.

VASILEVSKY ISLAND

Holiday Club $$$$ *Birzhevoy pereulok 2–4, tel: 812-335 2200, <www.holidayclub.fi>.* St Petersburg's newest and most atypical hotel is the Holiday Club, the city's first spa hotel. Built by Finns, the large hotel (with 278 rooms) is both sumptuous and new-age Nordic, with a modern soothing décor, luxuriously appointed bright rooms and every amenity a weary traveller could wish for. The spa and wellness centre is set to open in late 2008 with several pools, seven different types of sauna and an exhaustive range of spa treatments.

NashOtel (Our Hotel) $$$$ *11-aya liniya 50, tel: 812-323 2231, <www.nashotel.ru>.* If the Golden and Silver Ages of St Petersburg are not to your taste, you might enjoy NashOtel – a bright and modern anomaly among the city's largely retro hotel offerings. Built in 2006, the hotel has good-sized rooms filled with bright floral art, comfortable modern furnishings and bright-coloured sheets and pillows. It is located about five minutes from the Vasileostrovskaya metro station near the Spit. Breakfast not included.

Recommended Restaurants

In 1840, a St Petersburg newspaper recommended the following tour for visitors to the city: 'In the morning, drink coffee at the Admiralty corner of Nevsky prospekt, have breakfast by Police Bridge, lunch just past the Kazan Cathedral, and then have ice cream past Anichkov Bridge. In this way your stomach will complete a tour of Nevsky prospekt.' In today's St Petersburg you can do the same 'tour' – and in fact, visitors with all kinds of tastes and preferences can happily eat their way across the city. There are hundreds of cafés, coffee houses (like the consistently good Ideal Cup and Coffee Khaus), bliny shops, shawerma stands (gyros) and restaurants serving a variety of cuisines at a range of prices.

English-language publications (see page 122) can provide up-to-date listings of new eateries in the city. The list below includes some long-time favourites as well as some new restaurants and cafés that offer good food, service and ambience. The recommendations emphasise Russian cuisine as well as cuisine from the former Soviet republics, since St Petersburg is good place to try specialities from the Caucasus and Central Asia. As a guide, we have used the following symbols to give some idea of the cost of a three-course dinner for two. The prices are a US dollar average, with drinks.

$$$$	over US$80
$$$	US$50–80
$$	US$30–50
$	under US$30

NEAR THE ADMIRALTY

1913 $$ *Ulitsa Dekabristov 2, tel: 812-315 5148*. This restaurant has the clean and simple interior of a neighbourhood bistro, and offers good classic Russian cuisine from the year 1913, the last 'good' year in Russian history (before the start of World War I and the revolution). This is a great place to try Russian classics like 'herring under a fur coat', *solyanka* soup and handmade *pelmeni*. Good prices, large portions and friendly service.

Fasol (Bean) $$ *Gorokhovaya ulitsa 17, tel: 812-571 7454*. Fasol has a high-tech décor and international cuisine, with emphasis on the sunny climes of the Mediterranean: many light salads, grilled meats and fish, and pastas. The restaurant is popular among the designer and artistic crowd and puts on a really cheap prix-fixe business lunch.

Kavkaz $$ *Karavannaya Ulitsa 18, tel: 812-312 1665*. This simple and good restaurant serving Georgian food has been a favourite of locals for over a decade.

Kilikia $$ *Ulitsa Gorokhovaya, 26/40, tel: 812-327 2208*. This unpretentious Armenian café has a simple exposed brick interior and is usually filled with the local Armenian diaspora. The menu includes European dishes as well as excellent Armenian specialities, such as crunchy meatballs and richly spiced stews.

Khutor Vodograi $$ *Karavannaya ulitsa 2, tel: 812-570 5737*. This Ukrainian-themed restaurant, complete with costumed musicians, offers good, hearty Ukrainian specialities, including borscht, homemade sausages and сало (*salo*) (smoked pork fat served on black bread with a shot of pepper vodka).

Lya Rus $ *Konnogvardeysky bulvar 15, tel: 812-571 2946*. This small, rustic café near St Isaac's Cathedral is turning into a favourite local hang-out: the place where hungry Russians go for good cooking and ample portions. The café has a full restaurant menu offering dozens of salads, soups and mains. Everything tastes reassuringly home-made.

NEP Café $$–$$$ *Nab. reki Moiki 37, tel: 812-312 3722*. The NEP (New Economic Policy) recreates the café atmosphere of the 1920s, when Lenin allowed a bit of private enterprise. Excellent traditional and updated Russian cuisine with some innovative specialities, like ostrich marinated with kiwis and venison with juniper sauce. Fun cabaret show Wed–Sat starting at 8.30pm.

Receptoria $$$$ *Admiralteysky prospekt 10, tel: 812-312 7967*. This airy white restaurant overlooking the Admiralty is one of the city's finest. The French- and Italian-inspired cuisine is excellent and creative, with fresh terrines, pasta and risotto as well as exquisitely prepared and presented mains that change with the seasons. A small gourmet boutique sells artisanal French and Italian cheeses, pâté, savouries and sweets.

Russian Empire $$$$ *Nevsky prospekt 17, tel: 812-571 2409*. Is this the most elegant and expensive restaurant in Russia? In a restored section of the Stroganov Palace, sumptuous and rare French-influenced Russian cuisine is served on fine porcelain, with real silverware and Bohemian crystal.

Tolsty Fraer (Fat Friar) $–$$ *Kirpichny pereulok 1, tel: 812-314 5921*. This chain of pubs has outlets all over the city, and although the décor is definitely student bar, the food is cheap and surprisingly good. They have their own brews, which should be enjoyed traditionally with either boiled crayfish or сухарики (*sukhariki*), decadent garlicky fried bread. But their mains, like the handmade cutlets, are also tasty and satisfying (and cheap).

MID-NEVSKY PROSPEKT

Abrikosov Café $$ *Nevsky prospekt 40, tel: 812-312 2457*. This exquisite café from 1906 still has the original Chinese silk wall panels and old signs asking the patrons not to smoke. It looks like a tourist trap, but it actually has good café food (like double-decker smoked salmon sandwiches) and sumptuous cakes and pastries, at prices that are surprisingly affordable.

Aragvi $$–$$$ *Nab. reki Fontanki 9, tel: 812-570 5643*. The Aragvi provides a more elegant environment for enjoying excellent traditional Georgian cuisine. The whitewashed walls, fireplace and simple wooden furniture are pleasantly clean and warm, and the food, from the garlic-laden salads to the succulent *shashlyk*, is very good.

Baku $$$ *Ulitsa Sadovaya 12/23, tel: 812-941 3756*. If you'd like to step out of the Venice of the North into a sultan's palace, call in at this Azeri restaurant, with bright tiles, stained-glass windows and the warm colours of the south. The food is excellent, from rich salads to *plov* (pilaf) to *shashlyk*, especially the lamb.

Bliny Domik $ *Kolokolnaya ulitsa 8, tel: 812-315 9915.* This is the best of the bliny fast-food restaurants that have popped up around the city. You can get soups, salads and bliny with both sweet and savoury toppings, or *blinchiki* with a variety of fillings, prepared soft and doughy or fried and crisp. Friendly, fast, cheap and tasty.

Caviar Bar $$$$ *Mikhailovskaya ulitsa 1/7 (in the Grand Hotel Europe), tel: 812-329 6637.* For a decadent splurge, spend an evening in the Silver Age Caviar Bar, trying one – or more – of 70 kinds of vodka and one – or more – of three varieties of caviar. The bar also provides a business lunch and dinner menu featuring Russian and European classics.

Demidoff $$$$ *Nab. reki Fontanki 14, tel: 812-272 9181.* This upmarket restaurant with aristocratic 19th-century décor (including a working porcelain fireplace) is worth the expense. Demidoff serves traditional Russian haute cuisine with unusual twists, like salmon-stuffed *pelmeni* or duck roasted with honey, pine nuts, apples and fruit. Live music in the evenings.

Marius Pub $$ *Ulitsa Marata 11, tel: 812-315 4880.* This pub attached to the Helvetia Hotel has a cosy bar and eating area and a pleasant terrace. Both are open 24 hours a day, providing an expat- and tourist-friendly assortment of upmarket pub grub and Russian cuisine.

Metropol $ *Ulitsa Sadovaya 22, tel: 812-310 1875.* For generations, families have celebrated birthdays, school successes and other festive occasions at this delightful sweetshop. The Metropol's cakes, pastries and confectionery are a delicious hybrid of French and Viennese sweets and St Petersburg creativity. A pleasant place to stop for a midday pick-me-up.

Palkin $$$$ *Nevsky prospekt 47, tel: 812-703 5371.* The first Palkin tavern appeared in St Petersburg in 1785, and by the end of the 19th century there were several Palkin restaurants that were considered the finest eateries in the city. The last and best branch was closed in 1925, but in 2002, using photographs, archive material and advice from the Hermitage, Palkin opened once again at its former address. Despite the hype and prices, the décor is divine and the food is quite good: a felicitous blend of pre-revolutionary aristocratic cuisine and French-influenced contemporary dishes.

Podval Brodyachey Sobaki (The Stray Dog Cellar) $$–$$$ *Ploshchad Iskusstv 5/4, tel: 812-312 8047.* This basement café is a mecca for lovers of the Russian Silver Age. It was here that such luminaries as Osip Mandelstam and Anna Akhmatova read their poetry and sipped wine all through the night. Abandoned for decades, the site was slowly wheedled back from the city and opened once again as a café, art and performance centre. The walls are covered with art on exhibition, and there are performances (music, literary readings, jazz and folk music) every evening in one of the halls. The food is simple, ample and good Russian pub grub, some based on the original 1912 recipes (such as the tasty cutlets).

Triton $$$–$$$$ *Nab. reki Fontanki, 67–69, tel: 812-310 9449.* An expensive but excellent fish restaurant, with additional choices for both meat-lovers and vegetarians.

NEAR PLOSHCHAD VOSTANIYA

Bistrot Garcon $$$$ *Nevsky prospekt 95, tel: 812-717 2467.* The Bistrot Garcon is a cosy Parisian bistro dating from about 1945, with an antique ambience and chansons playing quietly in the background. The French chef prepares traditional and updated bistro fare, including terrines, fresh pastas and risottos, fanciful salads and such luxurious treats as duck filets with lime and lavender honey.

Chez Jules Café $$ *Ulitsa Gangutskaya 16, tel: 812-275 4953.* This tiny café near the Steiglitz Museum is French in ambience and multicultural in cuisine. It is a cosy and pleasant place with a prix-fixe menu that simply blends European and Russian traditions.

Molokhovets' Dream $$$$ *Ulitsa Radishcheva 10, tel: 812-929 2247.* At the turn of the 20th century, Elena Molokhovets wrote her *Gift for Young Homemakers,* an enormous volume filled with recipes and advice for young wives. Now most of these recipes are outdated, but a fine Russian chef has transformed the best of them into one of St Petersburg's finest dining experiences. The small restaurant has understated décor, excellent service and very good, subtly updated aristocratic Russian cuisine accompanied by quiet live music. This is the restaurant that Sir Paul McCartney favoured after his concert in the city.

TEATRALNAYA PLOSHCHAD AND KOLOMNA

Dvoryanskoe Gnezdo (Nest of the Nobility) $$$$ *Ulitsa Dekabristov 21, tel: 812-312 0911.* This restaurant, in a classical pavilion within the grounds of the Yusupov Palace, has a passionate following among the city's movers and shakers. With two menus, you can chose between classical Russian cuisine or the more 'Frenchified' cuisine of the nobility. Prices are high, but the formal ambience and excellent food are worth it.

Idiot $$ *Nab. reki Moiki 82, tel: 812-315 1675.* The Idiot is something of an expat legend: a warren of antique-filled and book-lined rooms serving vegetarian cuisine and lots of drinks (including a half-shot on the house just to get you going when you sit down).

Le'Chaim $$–$$$ *Lermontovsky prospekt 2, tel: 812-572 5616.* St Petersburg's only kosher restaurant has elegant décor and delicious food that ranges from the traditional (*latkes* and chicken schnitzel with mashed potatoes) to the more adventurous (lightly pickled salmon with arugula and fried trout with roast potatoes, caraway seeds and rosemary).

Okhotnichaya Izba (Hunter's Hut) $$ *Lermontovsky prospekt 30, tel: 812-714 6088.* This slightly kitsch rustic restaurant (complete with stuffed bear to greet guests) has a menu of traditional game as well as good Russian standards. Convenient after-performance dining near the Mariinsky Theatre.

Sadko Restaurant and Wine Bar $$$ *Ulitsa Glinka 2, tel: 812-920 8228*. After a night at the Mariinsky Theatre, this is a great place to have an excellent meal. Both its décor and cuisine are a pleasing blend of postmodernism and Russian tradition, from the austere grey tables and chairs and walls decorated with traditional Russian floral painting, to the *pelmeni* stuffed with venison or salmon. There are ample choices for vegetarians and a good wine list, including several surprisingly good Russian vintages.

OUTSIDE THE CITY CENTRE

Na Zdorovye! (To Your Health) $$–$$$ *Bolshoy prospekt 13/4, tel: 812-232 4039*. This cheerful *à la russe* restaurant is a good place on the Petrograd Side for hearty and simple Russian dishes (like *ukha*, a light fish soup) and Soviet-era favourites (like roasted veal steaks smothered with mushrooms, onions and cheese). There is live Russian and Roma music in the evenings.

Restoran $$$ *Tamozhenny pereulok 2, tel: 812-327 8979*. Housed in a former archive building, this restaurant has whitewashed vaulted ceilings, pine furniture and minimalist lighting. The cuisine is upmarket Russian: old recipes and traditional ingredients made startlingly new, like their herbal-fresh honey wine and 'Grandmother's Napoleon'. Call in for their excellent Russian buffet lunch or tea table.

Russkaya Rybalka $$$ *Yuzhnaya doroga 11, tel: 812-323 9813*. Located on an island where Prince Menshikov, Peter the Great's best friend, had his favourite fishing hole, you can fish in the pond and have the chef prepare your dish to order. As well as fun for kids, the food is quite good and elegant.

Troitsky Most $ *Kronverksky prospekt 35, tel: 812-326 8221*. There are a number of outlets of this vegetarian café around the city, all with the same cafeteria-style service as this one on the Petrograd Side. They offer about 10 salads (Russian and international), soups, mains and desserts. The portions are generous and the food satisfying. A good place for vegetarians craving some tofu or those who want a break from Russian cuisine.

INDEX

pocket guide

St Petersburg

First Edition 2008

Written by Michele A. Berdy
Edited by Anna Tyler
Series Editor: Tony Halliday

Photography credits
All photography by Anna Mockford and Nick Bonetti except: imagebroker/Alamy 89; Peter Titmuss/Alamy 97; Naki Kouyioumtzis/Axiom 9, 57, 86; Demianchuck/Reuters/Corbis 22; Günter Gräfenhain/SIME-4Corners Images 10, 82; Getty Images/National Geographic 103; Gudenko 16, 20; John Frumm/Hemis 85; Richard Nowitz 99; Tony Perrottet 100; Steve Raymer/Corbis 94.

Cover picture: Steve Vidler/SuperStock

Every effort has been made to provide accurate information in this publication, but changes are inevitable. The publisher cannot be responsible for any resulting loss, inconvenience or injury.

Printed in Singapore by Insight Print Services (Pte) Ltd, 38 Joo Koon Road, Singapore 628990. Tel: (65) 6865-1600. Fax: (65) 6861-6438

Berlitz Trademark Reg. U.S. Patent Office and other countries. Marca Registrada

Contact us

At Berlitz we strive to keep our guides as accurate and up to date as possible, but if you find anything that has changed, or if you have any suggestions on ways to improve this guide, then we would be delighted to hear from you.

Berlitz Publishing, PO Box 7910, London SE1 1WE, England.
fax (44) 20 7403 0290
email: berlitz@apaguide.co.uk
www.berlitzpublishing.com